UNIVERSITY OF ILLINOIS

THE NEED TO KNOW AND WHERE TO GO
GUIDE TO COLLEGE LIFE

Published by CGuides Media, 101 Forrest Crossing Boulevard, Suite 100, Franklin, TN 37064.

Library of Congress Control Number: 2007943975

First Printing, 2008
Printed in the United States
10 9 8 7 6 5 4 3 2 1

Campus Contributor: David Martinsek
Managing Editors: Doan Phuong Hoang Nguyen and Douglas N. Norfleet
Designer: Jay Smith, Juicebox Designs

Visit the CGuides Media Web site at www.cguides.net

http://uiuc.cguides.net

UNIVERSITY OF ILLINOIS

THE NEED TO KNOW AND WHERE TO GO
GUIDE TO COLLEGE LIFE

You made it! Welcome to the University of Illinois at Urbana-Champaign! You probably can't wait to leave your roots behind, but you'll soon develop new ones as your college years commence. With its boundless resources, campus may daunt you at first, but over time you will feel right at home as an Illini. And with this *CGuide* in hand, getting to know both the university and the Champaign-Urbana (C-U) community has never been easier.

This *CGuide* is intended to help you, the student, with your transition into college life. Inside these pages, you'll find everything you need for a smooth adjustment. Tips for everything from academics to food to entertainment options are at your disposal, making this book your one-stop shop for all that is the University of Illinois.

For the latest campus happenings, don't forget to visit the *CGuide* Web site at http://uiuc.cguides.net.

TABLE OF CONTENTS

5 WHERE TO EAT AND WHERE TO MEET 58

6 RECREATION, ENTERTAINMENT, AND THE ARTS 78

① CAMPUS LIFE
THE BASICS

Founded in 1867, Illinois's flagship campus was originally called Illinois Industrial University. The Urbana site was chosen following a contentious bidding process throughout the state to see which city would secure the land grant promised by the Morrill Act of 1862. The language of the act specified that the school would primarily be an industrial institution. This contrasted with the vision of John Milton Gregory, the university's first president, who advocated an approach based on liberal arts. Amid lawmakers' pressure for the school to live up to its industrial title, Gregory resigned in 1880, leaving the university's mission still cloudy. However, only five years later, the university established a multidisciplinary mission and was renamed the University of Illinois (*at Urbana-Champaign* was added in 1982).

Today, the university is led by Chancellor Richard Herman and President B. Joseph White (who also presides over the Chicago (UIC) and Springfield (UIS) campuses). A thirteen-member Board of Trustees and three student representatives, who are elected annually by each of the three campuses, exercise final authority over the university. In 2007, the Board of Trustees voted to remove the Chief Illiniwek symbol from athletic events, ending a hard-fought dispute regarding the potentially "hostile and abusive" representation of American Indians.

Since its inception, the U of I has remained one of the premier scientific institutions in the world, always at the helm of global change and technological advancement. Founders of worldwide superpower companies like BET, Netscape, and YouTube all have one thing in common—they sat in the very lecture halls that you will occupy.

Nestled in miles of cornfields, the Urbana-Champaign campus is a thriving cultural center unlike others. Whatever "Chambana" has in store for you—be it ethnic foods, music, plays, or rustic barn dances—experience it all. Late nights will be had in these twin cities—amid sonorous hangouts or

VITAL INFORMATION

UNIVERSITY OF ILLINOIS AT URBANA-CHAMPAIGN

901 W. Illinois St.
Urbana, IL 61801

MOTTO: Labor and learning

PUBLIC VS. PRIVATE: Public

ENDOWMENT: $1.4 billion (18.2% in state funds)

CAMPUS SIZE: 562 buildings on 4,805 acres.

WEB SITE: www.uiuc.edu

meticulous note regurgitation—but how you approach them will determine the quality of your stay.

You can find most stores conveniently located on Green Street, just off the Quad. And if you dare venture off campus, getting back is only a short bus ride away. A day trip to downtown could be what binds you with C-U. However, you first find yourself at home here on campus, so settle in and make new friends, eventually you too will bleed orange and blue.

STUDENT BODY MAKEUP

Although 88 percent of students at the university are Illinois residents, all fifty states and numerous foreign countries are represented throughout the different colleges. Illinois takes pride in celebrating the diverse roots of its students and recently launched the Inclusive Illinois initiative to further highlight cultural awareness through its "one campus, many voices" motto.

UNDERGRADUATE STUDENTS 30,935

GRADUATE STUDENTS 10,407

GENDER 53% Men 47% Women

MAJORS OFFERED

The University of Illinois offers around 120 major areas of study. To complete a major at UIUC, a student must take at least 120 hours, with core curriculum requirements varying across colleges.

FINDING YOUR MAJOR
If you aren't sure about what to study, you may want to major in general curriculum for your first two years. This Liberal Arts and Sciences (LAS) program gives students the flexibility to explore their interests within the entire university, so that they can find what they truly want to study. Students in general curriculum still must declare a major by the end of their sophomore year.

MINORS OFFERED

In all, 72 minors are available at the University of Illinois, but students must complete all required classes for a minor within a normal four-year window. In other words, no one can stay on campus simply to pursue a secondary concentration.

For information on majors and minors as well as links and contact information for each program of study, log on to http://courses.uiuc.edu/cis.

Registration dates for future semesters are doled out based on how many credit hours you have accrued at the university, with seniors selecting before freshmen, and so on. Exceptions do apply for Edmund J. James Scholars and honors students, but everyone uses the same Enterprise system found at https://apps.uillinois.edu.

If you discover a new field of interest that is in another college, try to take classes that regular majors from that school take. If you are involved on campus and maintain respectable grades, most colleges will allow you to apply for a transfer after your sophomore year. Even if you cannot transfer, for whatever reason, contact an advisor to see about a minor.

COLLEGES WITHIN THE UNIVERSITY

COLLEGE OF AGRICULTURAL, CONSUMER AND ENVIRONMENTAL SCIENCES (ACES)

Based on the agricultural industry for which Illinois is known, ACES offers 10 majors focused on land use improvement and food production processes. It is located in the southeast region of campus.
www.aces.uiuc.edu

COLLEGE OF APPLIED HEALTH SCIENCES (AHS)

With an emphasis on the human body, AHS has 4 undergraduate degree programs with focus ranging from public health to sports medicine to leisure management.
www.ahs.uiuc.edu

COLLEGE OF BUSINESS (BUS)

In preparing the leaders of tomorrow's global economy, BUS is divided into the departments of accountancy, business administration, and finance. Many students from other colleges take the same core classes as business students before transferring in after their sophomore year.
www.business.uiuc.edu

COLLEGE OF MEDIA (COM)

There are 3 majors in COM dealing with the different types of media in the ever-changing technological environment. Students cannot apply to the College of Media (formerly the College of Communications) until they have completed at least one semester of classes.
www.comm.uiuc.edu

COLLEGE OF EDUCATION (EDU)

A precursor to serving the educational needs of the future, EDU explores ways to revolutionize teaching through its three certification programs, which are each specific to different types of students: early childhood, elementary, and special education.
www.ed.uiuc.edu

COLLEGE OF ENGINEERING (ENGR)

Located on the Bardeen Quad, this college challenges students of its 14 majors to solve problems through interactive teamwork and to develop environmentally friendly designs. ENGR has consistently enjoyed high rankings among peer institutions.
www.engr.uiuc.edu

COLLEGE OF FINE AND APPLIED ARTS (FAA)

FAA houses 15 disciplines ranging from practical applications, such as designing cities and buildings, to strictly aesthetically pleasing painting and sculptural art forms.
www.faa.uiuc.edu

COLLEGE OF LIBERAL ARTS AND SCIENCES (LAS)

Everyone ends up taking a lot of classes in LAS, the catchall college, either to complete one of its 52 majors, fulfill general education requirements, or simply to learn a little more about an area of interest.
www.las.uiuc.edu

INSTITUTE OF AVIATION (AVI)

As the first Federal Aviation Administration-certified school for civilian pilot licenses, the Institute of Aviation examines how to make aircraft and air travel safer and more effective. www.aviation.uiuc.edu

TIP

Know where your college advising office is located. Meeting with an undergraduate advisor, even if you don't have any specific questions, can help you out in the long run. They're there to assist you, so consult them often.

● ATHLETICS

Illinois is best known for football and men's basketball and has enjoyed considerable success in other sports, such as gymnastics, soccer, tennis, and wrestling. Wherever you go, whatever sport is in season, you'll see students decked out in vibrant orange and blue supporting the Fighting Illini, no matter the win-loss record. For more information on Illini athletics, visit www.fightingillini.com.

CONFERENCE
Big Ten

MASCOT/SYMBOL
None (formerly Chief Illiniwek from 1926 to 2007)

COLORS
Orange and Blue

⊚ FIGHT SONGS

Like many schools, Illinois has more than one school song. "Oskee-Wow-Wow" is the official fight song and is often played by the Marching Illini with lyrics projected on the Memorial Stadium scoreboard, but most of the school spirit resides in the floor-shaking clap patterns that go along with the music. The only song students generally know the words to is the alma mater "Hail to the Orange." When it is sung at halftime, the students link arms and sway as part of the much-anticipated "Three in One" band routine.

The following second verse is not usually sung:

Teddy Roosevelt may be famous, and his name you often hear.
But it's heroes on the football field each college man holds dear.
We think with pride of Roberts, Artie Hall and Heavy, too.
Oskee-Wow-Wow for the wearers of the Orange and the Blue!

ILLINOIS LOYALTY

We're loyal to you Illinois,
We're Orange and Blue, Illinois,
We'll back you to stand 'gainst the best in the land,
For we know you have sand, Illinois, Rah! Rah!
So crack out that ball, Illinois,
We're backing you all, Illinois,
Our team is our fame protector,
Oh boys, for we expect a victory from you, Illinois!
Che-he! Che-ha! Che-ha-ha-ha! Go, Illini, Go!
Che-he! Che-ha! Che-ha-ha-ha! Go, Illini, Go!
Illinois! Illinois! Illinois!
Fling out that dear old flag of Orange and Blue,
Lead on your sons and daughters fighting for you,
Like men of old on giants placing reliance, shouting defiance
Oskee-Wow-Wow!
Amid the broad green plains that nourish our land,
For honest labor and for learning we stand,
And unto thee we pledge our heart and hand,
Dear Alma Mater, Illinois!

FIGHT SONG
Oskee-Wow-Wow

Old Princeton yells her tiger,
Wisconsin, her Varsity.
And they give the same old Rah Rah
Rah, at each university.
But the yell that always thrills me, and
fills my heart with joy,
is the good old Oskee-Wow-Wow, that
they yell at Illinois.
Os-kee-Wow-Wow, Illinois, Our eyes
are all on you.
Oskee-Wow-Wow, Illinois! Wave your
Orange and your Blue. Rah! Rah!

When the team
trots out before
you, Every man
stand up and yell,
Back the team to
victory, Os-kee-
Wow-Wow.
Illinois.

HAIL TO THE ORANGE

Hail to the Orange,
Hail to the Blue,
Hail Alma Mater,
Ever so true! (so true)
We love no other,
So let our motto be
Victory, Illinois! (the "s" is often sounded out) Varsity!

THE PRIDE OF THE ILLINI

We are marching for dear old Illini,
For the men who are fighting for you.
Here's a cheer for our dear Alma Mater,
May our love for her ever be true!
While we're marching along life's pathway,
May the spirit of old Illinois
Keep us marching and singing, with true Illini spirit,
For our dear old Illinois.

MEN'S TEAMS

- Baseball
- Basketball
- Cheerleading
- Cross Country
- Football
- Golf
- Gymnastics
- Tennis
- Track and Field
- Wrestling

WOMEN'S TEAMS

- Basketball
- Cheerleading
- Cross Country
- Golf
- Gymnastics
- Soccer
- Softball
- Swimming and Diving
- Tennis
- Track and Field
- Volleyball

"Although U of I is best known for men's basketball, the tennis, track and field, and wrestling teams are some of the more successful year in and year out. Plus, they're a lot cheaper and easier to get tickets for."

– TOM, Junior

◉ CAMPUS HOUSING

Freshmen who do not live at home must purchase room and board at either the university residence halls or through private certified housing. Although living in cramped quarters with someone you've never met may concern you, meeting people from different backgrounds is what college is all about. Sure residence hall life is sometimes hectic, but it's truly something no student should miss out on.

All units are staffed with trained resident advisors, and they offer many types of friendship-building outlets for students. For the many students who choose to get apartments after their freshman or sophomore years, the University Tenant Union is an invaluable tool for negotiating leases. They also maintain records on complaints against landlords, allowing prospective renters to be informed before signing a lease. Most apartments go on the market October 1st, so it's never too early to plan for next year.

For more housing information, log on to http://housing.uiuc.edu.

UNIVERSITY RESIDENCE HALLS

ALLEN HALL: UNIT ONE LIVING-LEARNING PROGRAM

Many students rave about Allen as the "artsy" place to stay, and it's not hard to see why. The Unit One program invites diverse guest speakers, sponsors entertaining events, and encourages students to take an active role in the hall's activities. Both men and women can live in Allen, which has mostly doubles. An auxiliary essay is required in the application process.

BUSEY-EVANS HALL

This elegant, air-conditioned facility houses only women. Demand for rooms is very high by both incoming and returning students. Like Allen, it features many specially designated study areas and provides free computer lab access to residents.

FLORIDA AVENUE RESIDENCE HALLS (FAR): OGLESBY AND TRELEASE

As the acronym implies, FAR is indeed quite separate from the rest of campus life. The twelve-story Oglesby and Trelease resemble high-rise hotels. Both men and women live in these packed, air-conditioned buildings.

GREGORY DRIVE RESIDENCE HALLS: FORBES, GARNER, HOPKINS, BARTON, AND LUNDGREN

As part of the "Six Pack" of coed halls, along with Peabody (yes, there are more than six in all), Gregory halls are favored by extroverted students because of their well-known high level of activity. The noise may get excessive at times, so many students go to the libraries to study. Tunnels interlock some of the halls on Gregory and Peabody drives; the tunnel spaces are primarily used by music groups or Registered Student Organizations.

ILLINOIS STREET RESIDENCE HALLS (ISR): TOWNSEND AND WARDALL

Probably the nicest and most sought-after housing, these two halls are located near the Bardeen Engineering Quad. Five-story Townsend is for men only, and twelve-story Wardall is primarily for women. Both buildings are air-conditioned. Student demand is often too great for the limited space of these well-kept destinations.

TIP

Get to know your roommate and be flexible about it! Make sacrifices and compromise as much as you can. But if problems do arise, switching rooms or halls isn't too much of a hassle.

LINCOLN AVENUE RESIDENCE HALLS (LAR): LEONARD AND SHELDON

This larger (as opposed to Busey-Evans) women-only complex offers a leadership development program for women. LAR is on the far eastern edge of university property, a considerable hike from the Quad. It has a reputation as one of the most poorly maintained areas of campus.

PEABODY DRIVE RESIDENCE HALLS: SCOTT, SNYDER, WESTON, AND TAFT-VAN DOREN

The other part of the Six Pack, Peabody Residence Halls are slightly closer to Memorial Stadium and Assembly Hall. Like Gregory Drive, both men and women live in each of these halls under the same set of rules. However, Snyder Hall has the added benefit of being the university's only substance-free hall, something that many residents seek out when applying to it. Weston provides the Exploration Living-Learning program to all residents.

PENNSYLVANIA AVENUE RESIDENCE HALLS (PAR): BABCOCK, BLAISDELL, CARR, AND SAUNDERS

Home to the Intersections and Global Crossroads Living-Learning Communities, PAR is a notch below Allen in terms of programming, but appears more like the other large residence hall complexes. Unfortunately, like many halls, Babcock, Blaisdell, Carr, and Saunders are not air-conditioned, something that may play a role in a student's selection, although they are generally regarded above FAR.

"Sign your lease or housing contract EARLY, and talk to someone who's lived there."

— MARIA, Sophomore

CAMPUS DINING

The university offers a wide array of dining options, ranging from kosher food to home-style food. Try not to eat at the same location every day; mix it up a little, so you don't burn out on campus food too fast. For weekly menus at the university dining locations, log on to www.housing.uiuc.edu/dining/menus.

DINING LOCATIONS

- **BUSEY BEANERY**
  1111 W. Nevada St.

- **BUSEY-EVANS**
  1111 W. Nevada St.

- **COCINA MEXICANA**
  1010 W. Illinois St.

- **CRACKED EGG CAFÉ**
  201 E. Gregory Dr.

- **FAT DON'S**
  Peabody-Snyder Dining Room
  206 E. Peabody Dr.

- **FIELD OF GREENS**
  LAR: North Dining Room
  1005 S. Lincoln Ave.

- **FLORIDA AVENUE RESIDENCE HALLS**
  1011 W. College Court

- **GREGORY DRIVE**
  201 E. Gregory Dr.

- **GREGORY E-CHOMPS**
  201 E. Gregory Dr.

- **ILLINOIS STREET RESIDENCE HALLS**
  1010 W. Illinois St.

ISR CHOMPS
1010 W. Illinois St.

KOSHER KITCHEN
Allen Dining Room
1005 W. Gregory Dr.

LINCOLN AVENUE AND ALLEN
1005 S. Lincoln Ave.

OODLES
1110 W. Nevada St.

PEABODY DRIVE
206 E. Peabody Dr.

SOUL INGREDIENT
1011 W. College Court

"Try one of the specialty restaurants on campus. They're good for breaking up the routine."

– STEVE, Junior

NUMBERS TO HAVE ON SPEED DIAL

Housing Information Office: **(217) 333-7111**

Campus telephone numbers: **(217) 333-1000**

Records Service Center: **(217) 333-0210**

② CAMPUS LIFE
THE DETAILS

The best way to make the University of Illinois *your* campus is to find activities or organizations to get involved with. These don't need to be strictly academic or athletic, but rather just something to help you build an identity and sense of belonging here. Whether through Panhellenic pledging, the various student organizations, or simple fan participation at the games, fellow students delightfully embrace new members with open arms. This is one of the biggest schools in the country, so pretty much anything you might be interested in has a related student organization. And if you can't find one, creating a new club isn't a hassle at all!

◉ GREEK LIFE

Illinois has the largest Greek system in the nation with 97 chapters in all, 37 sororities and 60 fraternities. More than 6,000 students and 22 percent of all undergrads are involved in the Greek community. Because so many students participate in Greek life, spaces in the various houses are very limited, so it is not uncommon for members to commute from other residences.

Sororities go through formal recruitment, primarily by way of the Internet. In this multifaceted process, prospective new members (PNMs) visit all Panhellenic chapters and slowly narrow down their choices before Bid Day, the culmination of rush week.

By contrast, fraternities bring in new members through less-structured pledge events, like cookouts accompanied by light recreational activities, ranging from backyard baseball and dodgeball to Ultimate Frisbee and wrestling.

All 4 Greek councils (Black Greek, Interfraternity, Panhellenic, and United Greek) and their members volunteer actively in the community and support charity through creative fundraising efforts. More than one-third of the chapters at Illinois are culturally based.

For information on all that is Greek, visit www.illinigreeks.com and www.odos.uiuc.edu/greek.

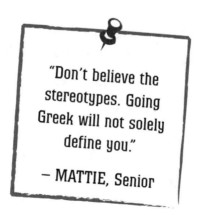

"Don't believe the stereotypes. Going Greek will not solely define you."

– MATTIE, Senior

⦿ CLUBS AND ORGANIZATIONS

Essentially, every possible extracurricular activity can be found on campus. There are more than 800 Registered Student Organizations (RSO) at Illinois. If you can't find what you're interested in, you can apply to create your own RSO. Unlike private organizations, RSOs are able to tap into student activity fees in order to fund their events.

The complete list of RSOs is available at www.union.uiuc.edu/involvement/rso.

A CAPPELLA

If you're interested in singing a cappella, there are a variety of vocal groups you can join. The most popular are the all-female groups The Girls Next Door and The Rip Chords and the all-male groups The Other Guys and The Xtension Chords A Capella Singers.

MEDIA PUBLISHING

Interested in media? You have a multitude of options. As the independent news source for the university, Illini Media encompasses *The Daily Illini* newspaper, *Illio* yearbook, *Technograph* journal, and WPGU 107.1 FM radio. For students interested in expressing conservative and libertarian ideas, check out the alternative publication, *Orange and Blue Observer*. The area is also home to the Independent Media Center's Urbana-Champaign chapter, which produces and distributes media and art for WRFU 104.5 FM and for various small publications.

MUSIC PRODUCTION

There are several clubs on campus involved in music marketing, including Green St. Records, which compiles the best music on campus, and Star Course, which takes care of everything from booking to ushers for the well-known acts it brings to campus.

POLITICAL ORGANIZATIONS

Most every political persuasion has a voice at UIUC, from College Democrats and College Republicans to social outreach programs like Campus Antiwar Network and Students for Social Equality.

STUDENT GOVERNMENT

Illinois Student Senate (www.iss.uiuc.edu) serves as the official voice of the student population. Each college elects its own senators, and they work in conjunction with university officials and the city councils to represent student interests.

RELIGIOUS ORGANIZATIONS

Numerous groups for different faiths exist on campus, including Campus Crusade for Christ, a nondenominational Christian group; Chabad Jewish Student Association, the official voice of the Jewish population; Greek InterVarsity, a Christian fellowship for Panhellenic students; the Muslim Students Association, a network uniting followers of Islam across campus; and Fellowship of Catholic University Students, a group that connects Catholics through discussion. These listings are by no means comprehensive. All religions offer a variety of programs to worshippers.

INTRAMURALS

Intramural sports satisfy students wishing to continue athletics or to try their hand at a new competition. Many sports are offered, from football to extreme triathlons and broomball at the University of Illinois Ice Arena. Men's, women's, and corecreational divisions are usually available. Fees are under $100 and cover referees, scheduling, and equipment.

Leagues are often loosely defined by residence or simply a group of friends. The eligibility rules are generally flexible. Mostly it's about having fun, at least at the residence hall level.

Fraternities have their own competitive leagues that are split into two groups, depending on the size of house membership. To a lesser extent, sororities may play against one another or against other all-female groups who are not involved in Greek life.

All information on intramural sports, from organizing a league to fees to registration dates and meetings, can be found at www.campusrec.uiuc.edu/intramurals.

CLUB SPORTS

Largely because of Title IX, which mandates equal opportunity in school athletic departments, a need arose on large campuses for competitive club sports, albeit not under scholarship or on the varsity level. The most notable among these are the Illinois men's hockey team and both men's and women's wheelchair basketball teams, which number among the nation's best squads on the club circuit year in and year out. In general, club sports are very hard to participate in, but tryouts do occasionally take place.

CONFERENCE ATHLETICS

FAN EXPERIENCE

At Illinois, numerous sports are always in season, inundating fans with a wealth of diverse and competitive teams. Although you'll find the largest seas of orange at home football and men's basketball games, securing tickets has perennially been a problem during successful times. Whether or not students attend those events, they can explore athletics with smaller followings by arriving for a home game and buying cheaper tickets with closer seats.

FOOTBALL

Since 1910, "Block I" has existed at home football games to provide the student body with a recognizable place in the stands. Today Block I seats are located in the south endzone and east stands. At each halftime, the section creates "card stunts" where each member holds up a card to collectively display symbols of school pride that are visible across Memorial Stadium.

BASKETBALL

Orange Krush, the student support group for men's basketball, also raises money for local charities through fundraising. Although the student section dates back to 1975, the foundation was not adopted until 1997. Krush members line the Assembly Hall floor at home games and are recognized as one of the most vocal cheering sections in the country.

"Block I at football games is an experience every Illini should have."

– KRISTEN, Sophomore

SECURING TICKETS

Ticket order forms are mailed to all incoming freshmen, but students can also call or go online to purchase seats. Block I vouchers are sold at a discounted rate to students, beginning in the summer, with a valid i-card. Season vouchers can be exchanged for tickets on game day so that students can sit with friends. Every member of Block I automatically joins Illini Pride and receives a free T-shirt.

Ask your neighbors to pledge money for each three-pointer the Illini score this season. Higher levels of giving translate to greater benefits; All-American status includes free season tickets, priority seating, and the first opportunities to buy seats for the annual Braggin' Rights game against Missouri in St. Louis, games at the United Center in Chicago, and possible NCAA Tournament contests. Tickets go fast!

HOW TO SECURE TICKETS

For more information, visit www.illinipride.com or the Illini Pride cubicle in the Illini Union.

To purchase single game or student-rate season tickets, contact the Athletic Ticket Office by e-mail at illinitickets@uiuc.edu or call either (217) 333-3470 or (866) ILLINI-1.

PAINT THE HALL

The consummate representation of the Illinois fan experience is the annual "Paint the Hall Orange" game at Assembly Hall which began in 2000. Despite this tradition's recent arrival, it has played host to several crucial matchups, among them Illinois's 91-73 victory against then-No. 1 ranked Wake Forest in 2004, which culminated with a 37-2 record and Final Four appearance.

"Join Orange Krush! You'll thank me later."

— JAKE, Junior

⊛ LIBRARIES

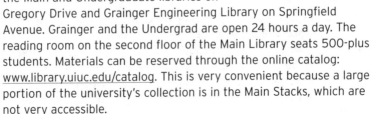

The university houses the largest public university library in the nation, with more than 10 million volumes spread across its various locations. The largest buildings are the Main and Undergraduate libraries on Gregory Drive and Grainger Engineering Library on Springfield Avenue. Grainger and the Undergrad are open 24 hours a day. The reading room on the second floor of the Main Library seats 500-plus students. Materials can be reserved through the online catalog: www.library.uiuc.edu/catalog. This is very convenient because a large portion of the university's collection is in the Main Stacks, which are not very accessible.

MAIN LIBRARY

With the largest collection of materials on campus, this spacious building holds a number of discipline-specific or niche libraries, including the Rare Book and Manuscript Library. The reference desk here is never cramped, and plenty of terminals are available for student use, even though this library is used by all undergraduates, grad students, and faculty.

> 1408 W. Gregory Drive
> Phone: (217) 333-2290
> Circulation Hours: Monday–Thursday, 8:30 a.m. - 11 p.m.
> Friday, 8:30 a.m. - 6 p.m.
> Saturday, 11 a.m. - 5 p.m. &
> Sunday, 1 p.m. - 11 p.m.

GRAINGER ENGINEERING LIBRARY

This mostly donated venue is located in the heart of the Engineering Quad, although many students from other colleges come for the comfy couches and state-of-the-art media resources. Grainger's secluded study rooms are perfect for late-night study sessions.

> 1301 W. Springfield Ave.
> Phone: (217) 333-3576
> Hours: Open Sunday 10 a.m. - Close
> Friday 9 p.m. &
> Saturday, 10 a.m. - 9 p.m.

UNDERGRADUATE LIBRARY

Buried underground, this student-friendly library was not built to protect the Morrow Plot cornstalks from the sun as commonly thought. In any event, the Undergrad is very much a marketplace of learning with a central courtyard letting light in from above. Computers are harder to come by here, and everyone and their mother seems to show up on Sundays and during finals week, so the noise level and atmosphere may not be conducive to learning.

> 1402 W. Gregory Drive
> Phone: (217) 333-3477
> Hours: Open Sunday, 10 a.m. - Close
>   Friday, 10 a.m. - 10 p.m. &
>   Saturday, 10 a.m. - 10 p.m.

Major library locations and hours are found at www.library.uiuc.edu/services/hours.php.

BRINGING BOOKS HOME

A valid i-card is required to check out materials, but the larger libraries all offer several free terminals with Internet access as well as study rooms with televisions and audio/video players available by request. On occasion, an instructor (or the library, for more precious items) will place documents on reserve, but the online library provides full-text versions of most journal articles. In addition, the university subscribes to dozens of databases that can be accessed with a NetID and password.

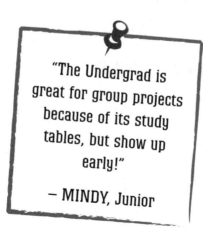

"The Undergrad is great for group projects because of its study tables, but show up early!"

— MINDY, Junior

CAMPUS DETAILS

OTHER PLACES TO STUDY

ESPRESSO ROYALE CAFÉ
The quintessential campus coffee shop, the ERC fosters learning, and some students swear they work better in the rich ambience of brews than the silence at home. Wi-Fi is generally available at all locations; the two most popular are inside the Undergrad itself and across from the Krannert Center for the Performing Arts.

1402 W. Gregory Drive
Phone: (217) 333-7799
Hours: Monday–Thursday, 8 a.m. – midnight
Friday, 8 a.m. – 6 p.m.
Saturday, 11:30 a.m. – 6 p.m. &
Sunday, 1:30 p.m. – midnight
1117 W. Oregon St.
Phone: (217) 333-6160
Hours: Daily, 7 a.m. – midnight

MOONSTRUCK FINE CHOCOLATE CAFÉ
Like Espresso Royale, Moonstruck creates a tranquil atmosphere in which students can study. Additionally, its desserts are full of sugar that will keep you up all night so you can study for that midterm tomorrow.

709 S. Wright St.
Phone: (217) 367-7402
Hours: Monday–Friday, 7 a.m. – 11 p.m. &
Saturday & Sunday, 9 a.m. – 11 p.m.

COMPUTER LABS

Campus Information Technologies and Educational Services (CITES) labs:

ENGLISH BUILDING
608 S. Wright St., Room 8
Hours: Monday–Thursday, 8 a.m. – midnight
Friday, 8 a.m. – 8 p.m.
Saturday, noon – 10 p.m.
Sunday, noon – midnight

ILLINI UNION

1401 W. Green St., Room 187

Hours: Monday–Thursday, 8 a.m. – midnight
Friday, 8 a.m. – 10 p.m.
Saturday, 10 a.m. – 10 p.m.
Sunday, noon – midnight

*NEVADA BUILDING

1203 1/2 W. Nevada St.

Hours: Monday–Friday, 8 a.m. – 8 p.m.
Saturday & Sunday, noon – 8 p.m.

*OREGON LAB

901 W. Oregon St.

Hours: Monday–Thursday, 8 a.m. – midnight
Friday 8 a.m. – 8 p.m.
Saturday, noon – 8 p.m.
Sunday, noon – midnight

*UNDERGRADUATE LIBRARY LAB

1402 W. Gregory Drive, Upper NE corner

Hours: Monday–Thursday, 8 a.m. – 3 a.m.
Friday, 8 a.m. – 10 p.m.
Saturday, 10 a.m. – 10 p.m.
Sunday, 10 a.m. – 3 a.m.

*WOHLERS HALL LAB

1206 S. Sixth St., Room 70 A/B

Hours: Monday–Thursday, 8 a.m. – midnight
Friday, 8 a.m. – 6 p.m.
Saturday, noon – 6 p.m.
Sunday, noon – midnight

*used for academic classes and may not be available at some times

Numerous buildings on campus are UIUCnet Wi-Fi enabled. So if you're carrying around a laptop, it's a good bet you'll be able to find a connection.

CAMPUS DETAILS

COPY CENTERS

Students may print up to a certain number of pages at university labs or libraries. For advanced printing needs and professional help, these stores are useful:

DEAN'S SUPERIOR BLUEPRINT
404 E. University Ave.
Phone: (217) 359-3261

FEDEX KINKO'S
613 S. Wright St.
Phone: (217) 398-0003

STAPLES
2005 N. Prospect Ave.
Phone: (217) 373-8490

UPCLOSE PRINTING AND COPIES
714 S. Sixth St.
Phone: (217) 384-7474

PARKING

Because it's often a hassle, many students do not bring a car to campus, especially with parking at a premium. Lots E-14, F-23, B-22, and North Deck B04 are available to student renters, but spaces go fast and the Parking Department is quick to ticket offenders who are parked illegally.

However, after 5 p.m. in most places, street parking is free. Parking overnight, either in the garages or on several of the residential streets bordering campus, is prohibited and will result in towing.

For more information or to purchase a hang tag, visit www.parking.uiuc.edu.

⊛ TRANSPORTATION

The University contracts with the Champaign-Urbana Mass Transit District (C-U MTD or MTD) to provide frequent state-of-the-art shuttles across campus for extended hours.

Visit www.cumtd.com for complete MTD routes and schedules, including weekend and special bus services. Here are the routes taken most often by university students:

22 ILLINI
This route covers the campus hot spots and runs every 10 minutes during school days. It also shuttles to FAR, PAR, ISR, and Orchard Downs graduate housing.

24 SOUTH CAMPUS
This complement to the 22 Illini runs roughly every 20 minutes on days when class is in session and visits less-frequented areas of campus like the agricultural complex and Arboretum. It also shuttles to LAR and PAR.

2 RED
Extending to the commercial areas of Chambana, the 2 Red (or 20 Red as it's known on weekends) runs roughly every 25 minutes on weekdays and goes to Marketplace Mall, Beverly Cinema, and the Prospect Avenue shopping district. It's a free way to get some shopping in.

5 GREEN
This line visits downtown Urbana, particularly Lincoln Square Mall, Boardman's Art Theatre, and the Virginia Theatre. It runs roughly every half hour on weekdays.

SAFETY ON CAMPUS

The university is policed by the Champaign, University, and Urbana police departments. Student patrol teams and campus police officers randomly patrol Campustown streets, facilities, and parking lots late at night.

CALL BOXES

Emergency telephones, stationed around campus and recognizable by their blue lights, give students the opportunity to report emergencies as they are taking place when a phone is otherwise unavailable. They can be used at any time, and the line is always staffed.

SAFERIDES

C-U MTD also runs this complimentary program intended to safely chauffeur students to their residences and other campus locations late at night. SafeRides does not drive students to bars or hospitals. Excessive use while intoxicated will result in a ban from future rides. Call (217) 265-RIDE for more information or to be picked up.

SAFEWALKS

The SafeWalks program, like SafeRides, is a means for students to safely travel at night. To arrange a SafeWalk, call (217) 333-1216. SafeWalk hours are Sunday–Thursday, 9 p.m. – 2 a.m.; Friday-Saturday, 9 p.m. – 3 a.m.

PEDESTRIAN SAFETY

Numerous accidents have forced the university to adopt a comprehensive pedestrian safety program for freshmen. Buses are equipped with proactive warning systems, but pedestrians should take every precaution when crossing roadways. University police officers cite jaywalking students with warnings to enforce this crucial safety concern, and repeat offenders may be ticketed and/or fined.

SAFETY WORKSHOPS

All freshmen are required to take ACEIT and FYCARE workshops to educate them on alcohol and drug awareness and sexual violence. The Whistle-Stop Program distributes whistles to all new female students. The whistles, when sounded, protect victims by drawing attention to criminal acts. Rape Aggression Defense (RAD) courses for women give them strategies for fighting off rape or robbery when help is not nearby.

PUBLIC SAFETY BUILDING

1110 W. Springfield Ave.

Hours: 24 hours a day.

Phone: (217) 333-1216 for regular questions,
and 9-1-1 for emergencies.

To call in a tip for an ongoing investigation, call Crimestoppers at (217) 373-TIPS.

To report or get counseling for a rape, call the Rape Crisis Hotline at (217) 355-5203.

CAMPUS DETAILS

The university's 24-hour general counseling and assistance hotline is (217) 359-4141.

General safety tips to avoid becoming the victim of a crime:

- Always keep your doors and windows locked, even if you are still inside.

- Tell a friend where and with whom you'll be and when you'll be back.

- Trust your instincts—if you feel uncomfortable on the street, in an elevator, or getting off a bus, head for a populated place or yell for help.

- Use well-lit and busy sidewalks.

- Drink responsibly—remember, your ability to respond is diminished by alcohol.

- Never leave personal property (e.g., book bags, laptops, phones, etc.) unattended.

- Lock car doors and roll up the windows, even if you're only running a fast errand.

- Stay alert at all times and call the police immediately to report suspicious activity.

For more safety tips and information on crime prevention programs, visit www.dps.uiuc.edu.

For policies concerning severe weather events or emergencies, ask resident advisors.

TRADITIONAL CAMPUS EVENTS

CAMPUS REC BLOCK PARTY

As part of Welcome Week activities, the Division of Campus Recreation sponsors this free indoor/outdoor event and opens up the recreation centers to all takers, providing copious free foods and sweet giveaways.

QUAD DAY

If you're a freshman, you should go to this right before classes start. All (or most) of the Registered Student Organizations line the Quad and distribute fliers to prospective members. You won't glean much information from these brief interactions and you may sign up for one too many e-mail lists, but something may catch your eye here that wouldn't otherwise.

TASTE OF NEVADA STREET FESTIVAL

This annual August event is an opportunity for the four cultural houses on campus to display what's unique about their programs and to attract new members. This celebration is more like a pep rally than other university-sponsored events and features dishes from around the world as well as informative tours about resources for minorities.

STUDY ABROAD FAIR

The university has one of the best study abroad programs in the world and lets students take their curricular responsibilities to scores of distinct locales. Here you can talk one-on-one with representatives from each program/location offered and find out what separates it from the rest. Companies look for individuals who have faced the rigors of adjustment that come with studying in a foreign country. Plus, it's a new experience, maybe cheaper than campus, and just might change you. It's never too early to think about going abroad because the application process takes time.

WALL TO WALL GUITAR FESTIVAL

This biennial multiday event is dedicated to the rich history and globalization of the guitar and shouldn't be missed. In past events, the chancellor has even rocked out Johnny Cash–style on Guitar Hero!

DADS WEEKEND

This October weekend is dedicated to the patriarchs who have gotten students here and probably paid many of the bills along the way. Show Dad what you've become involved in so far and rekindle your intimate bond at the Dads' Day football game where King Dad is crowned.

HOMECOMING

While not as big a deal at Illinois as other schools, Homecoming is still rich with plentiful opportunities. Be a part of the Homecoming Court or vote one of your friends in. Highlights also include iHelp: A Homecoming Volunteer Project and the featured football game at Memorial Stadium.

PAINT THE HALL ORANGE GAME

This February game may not seem different from any other home basketball game, but it is. The usual sea of orange encircles Assembly Hall, but this time it's for the most charged home game of the season, often against a bitter conference rival. Vest yourself in orange and be true to your school, showing how overpowering a home-court advantage can be!

MOMS WEEKEND

Unlike Dads Weekend, this one has a little more structure. Take time out for Mom. She misses you. A number of arts and crafts fairs are available, and many students take their moms out to remind them of their distant college years.

NUMBERS TO HAVE ON SPEED DIAL

Campus information desk: **(217) 333-4666**

SafeRides: **(217) 265-RIDE**

C-U MTD (for routes and times):
(217) 384-8188

Library Reference Desk: **(217) 333-2290**

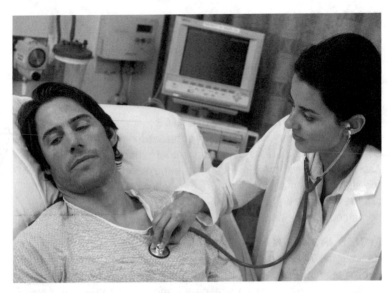

③ TO YOUR HEALTH

Keeping healthy away from home can be difficult, which is why it's important to be aware of the health services that are provided by the university. From flu shots and regular checkups to visits with specialists and preparations for traveling abroad, the campus health services provide it all. When you're feeling under the weather, it's a good idea to get things checked out before it gets serious and hampers your life at school, especially because you may not be sleeping as much as you're used to.

CAMPUS HEALTH CLINIC

The McKinley Health Center serves the University of Illinois with a variety of services that the Health Service Fee (part of the enrollment fee) helps to prepay. McKinley provides a 24-hour Dial-A-Nurse service, visits with your primary care provider, pharmacy service, mental health services, travel exams and inoculations, a Women's Health Clinic, Health Resource Centers with over-the-counter supplies, and health and wellness information from the Health Education Unit.

TO YOUR HEALTH

MCKINLEY HEALTH CENTER

1109 S. Lincoln Ave.

Hours: Most departments in the hospital are open from 8 a.m. – 5 p.m. On Saturday, the Medical Clinic is open 8 a.m. – 4:30 p.m.; and the pharmacy is open from 8:30 a.m. – 12:30 p.m. & 1:30 p.m. – 4:30 p.m. The clinic is closed on Sunday.

In any emergency, dial 9-1-1 (9-911 from campus phones). During regular business hours at McKinley, you can reach the following services at these numbers:

- Administration: (217) 333-2711
- Business Office: (217) 333-2719
- Cancellations: (217) 244-6066
- Dial-A-Nurse: (217) 333-2700
- East 1 Clinic: (217) 265-0703
- Immunization and Travel Clinic: (217) 333-2702
- General Information: (217) 333-2701
- Health Education: (217) 333-2714
- Health Resource Center at McKinley: (217) 333-6000
- Health Resource Center at the Union: (217) 244-5994
- HIV Testing Appointments: (217) 333-2700
- Immunization Questions: (217) 333-2702
- Management Information Services: (217) 244-5661
- Medical Clinic Appointments: (217) 333-2700
- West 1 Clinic: (217) 333-2700
- West 2 Clinic: (217) 333-2700
- Medical Records: (217) 333-2700
- Mental Health: (217) 333-2705
- Pharmacy: (217) 333-2710
- Prescription Refill: (217) 244-2511

- Radiology: (217) 333-2752
- SportWell Center: (217) 244-0261
- TTY Phone: (217) 244-5723
- Women's Health: (217) 333-2700

⚙ LOCAL HOSPITALS

While the campus health center covers most services for students, emergency care is provided by area hospitals, Carle Foundation Hospital and Provena Covenant Medical Center. Call 9-1-1 (9-911 from a campus phone) for an ambulance that will take you to either hospital.

Carle and Provena are also available for nonemergency visits, such as regular checkups and appointments with specialists. Both are ranked very highly by accreditation agencies, but Carle has larger facilities. Most visits to hospitals, like emergency room trips when your roommate accidentally cuts his hand on a fruit can lid, are unplanned. If you are able to plan in advance, investigate both options before undergoing a procedure to see which provides superior service and is more cost-effective for your budget.

CARLE FOUNDATION HOSPITAL
611 W. Park St.
Patient Information Line: (217) 383-3311
Registration Center: (217) 383-3031
Business Office and Patient Accounts Services: (217) 326-2900
Provena Covenant Medical Center
1400 W. Park St.
General Information Line: (217) 337-2000
PRO Ambulance and Medi-van: (217) 337-2911
Emergency Department: (217) 337-2131
Home Health Care Center: (217) 337-2433
Pharmacy: (217) 337-4545

⚙ GENERAL DOCTORS

Suppose you need to prove your clean bill of health in order to study abroad. Get a quick, comprehensive physical at any local health clinic. It's best to shy away from the hospitals because things can get intense there; clinics are usually unhurried spaces designed to make patients feel right at home.

McKinley Health Center's Medical Clinics provide primary medical care to students. There are three separate clinics (two in the west building of the health center, and one in the east building) where students can make appointments, either by calling the Dial-A-Nurse line, (217) 333-2700, 24 hours a day, 7 days a week, or online at www.mymckinley.com.

Carle Clinic, 1802 South Mattis Avenue in Champaign, has several general practitioners on staff, including Drs. Joyce Beitel, David Conner, Bharat Gopal, Dawn McCoy, Mahtab Tashakori, and Stanley Wu, as well as nurse practitioners Laura Parrett and Marcia Zukosky. Appointments can be made by calling (217) 326-1330.

⦿ WOMEN'S HEALTH

McKinley also has a Women's Health Clinic that provides preventive care and the treatment and management of health-related issues, with an emphasis on reproductive health. Services offered at the center include routine annual exams, contraception, sexually transmitted infection screening and treatment, breast exams, and pregnancy options counseling. The Women's Health Clinic is open Monday–Friday, 8 a.m. – 5 p.m., and appointments can be scheduled through the Dial-A-Nurse line.

If McKinley is closed or unavailable, try Carle. They may be able to fit you in with enough notice, and the doctors there are very knowledgeable about women's health issues from Pap tests to pregnancy counseling.

DRS. MICHAEL DAY, AMANPREET SETHI, DEBORAH SINGLETON, JEFFREY SWEARINGEN, AND DAVID WHITEHILL
602 W. University Ave.
Phone: (217) 383-3311

DRS. INES BAQUERO, MELINDA DABROWSKI, THEODORE FRANK, AND REBECCA WAGNER EXPERT NURSES KATHLEEN EASTER AND MARTY GUYON
1813 W. Kirby Ave.
Phone: (217) 326-1200

DR. SUZANNE TRUPIN
2125 S. Neil St.
Phone: (217) 356-2736

◉ EYE DOCTORS

The Carle team of ophthalmologists
and optometrists are among the most
skilled in the area, but appointments are often hard to get, and
student fees do not cover them. For lightning-quick service when
your glasses break or your contacts fall out, walk in to Lens Crafters
at the mall, the one-stop shop for eye care from exams to fittings.

DRS. DAVID ELLIS, JAMES FARON, DAVID JOHNSON, THOMAS MALEE, SCOTT OHL, AND JOHN WILLIAMS
602 W. University Ave.
Phone: (217) 383-3311

LENS CRAFTERS
2000 N. Neil St.
Phone: (217) 356-8585

JONES OPTICAL CO.
1711 S. Neil St.
Phone: (217) 359-2390

◉ DENTISTS

Both Carle Clinic and Provena Medical Center perform oral and
maxillofacial surgery, but neither has a regular staff of dentists on
hand for routine checkups. Although she is far from campus, the 2 Red
bus route will take you to Dr. Cheng, who has a glowing reputation for
treating patients kindly and operating in nonintrusive ways.

DR. CHIFAN CHENG
1211 E. Colorado Ave.
Phone: (217) 337-6000

DR. RICHARD BLANCO
101 W. University Ave.
Phone: (217) 366-1246

DRS. JEFFREY BRUNSON, WILLIAM THOMPSON, DONALD JANOFF, ALLEN MCCALL, AND CASEY DANKLE
507 S. Second St.
Phone: (217) 352-9688

⊙ COUNSELING SERVICES

Maybe you're going through a rough patch in your life or a test has you really stressed- out. General counseling is already paid for in student fees! McKinley Health Center has a fully staffed Mental Health Clinic with trained experts to sensitively deal with whatever afflicts you. Although the counseling is free, you may need to make a small co-pay for prescription drugs. For an appointment, call (217) 333-2705. In case of an emergency after hours, call the Champaign County Mental Health Center Crisis Line at (217) 359-4141.

"The one thing about McKinley is that they don't cover everything, so you need to either keep your specialists at home or find doctors at Carle or Provena."

— MARY, Senior

NUMBERS TO HAVE ON SPEED DIAL

Dial-A-Nurse at McKinley (schedule appointments, 24 hours a day): **(217) 333-2700**

Carle General Information: **(217) 383-4636**

Carle Patient Advisory Nurse (schedule appointments): **(217) 383-3233**

Provena General Information: **(217) 337-2000**

TO YOUR HEALTH

⊕④ LOCAL SERVICES
SURVIVING ON YOUR OWN

Although you'll spend most of your college career on campus, the city you're in also plays a part in your life at school. You hope you'll never have to use these numbers, but knowing how to reach emergency services is vital to your safety. Other local services, such as banks and post offices, are very important to college life as well.

POLICE, FIRE, AND RESCUE

UNIVERSITY OF ILLINOIS POLICE DEPARTMENT
1110 W. Springfield Ave.
Phone: (217) 333-2337 (or 3-2237 from a campus phone)
Nonemergency calls: (217) 333-1216
Emergency: 9-1-1 (9-911 from a campus phone)

CHAMPAIGN CITY POLICE DEPARTMENT
82 E. University Ave.
Phone: (217) 351-4545.
Emergency: 9-1-1 (9-911 from a campus phone)

URBANA POLICE DEPARTMENT
400 S. Vine St.
Phone: (217) 384-2321
Emergency: 9-1-1 (9-911 from a campus phone)

CHAMPAIGN FIRE DEPARTMENT HEADQUARTERS
307 S. Randolph St.
Emergency: 9-1-1 (9-911 from a campus phone)

URBANA FIRE RESCUE SERVICES
400 S. Vine St.
Emergency: 9-1-1 (9-911 from a campus phone)

CARROLL FIRE PROTECTION DISTRICT
1811 N. Brownfield Road
Emergency: 9-1-1 (9-911 from a campus phone)

⊙ BANKS

Bank locations on campus are somewhat limited, but there are three options right near the center of campus, all very close to the intersection of Green and Sixth Streets. Busey is probably the best option because of its many locations and the fact that it has strong local roots, so you know who to call if a problem arises. National City's reputation precedes it as well. You really can't go wrong with a bank as long as it's convenient enough for you.

NATIONAL CITY BANK
    505 E. Green St. #2
    Phone: (217) 363-4080
    Hours: Monday–Friday, 9 a.m. - 5 p.m. &
            Saturday, 9 a.m. - noon

BUSEY BANK
    614 S. Sixth St.
    Phone: (217) 365-4552
    Hours: Monday–Friday, 9 a.m. - 5 p.m. &
            Saturday, 9 a.m. - noon.
            A 24-hour ATM is available outside.

FREESTAR BANK
    631 E. Green St.
    Phone: (217) 351-6688
    Hours: Monday–Friday 9 a.m. - 5 p.m. &
            Saturday 9 a.m. - noon.

"Busey Bank has great free checking for students, and since they're right in the middle of campus, it's really convenient."

– KATIE, Sophomore

LAUNDROMATS AND DRY CLEANERS

There are numerous washing machines available in each residence hall, but if they're booked or you're tired of separating your whites from colors and want a truly professional laundromat, there are a number of options available. Personal Touch Laundromat or Garber's Cleaners are probably the best choices because they are so close to campus.

COUNTRY SQUIRE CLEANERS
1805 W. Springfield Ave.
Phone: (217) 356-9422
Hours: Monday–Friday, 7 a.m. – 8 p.m. &
Saturday, 7 a.m. – 6 p.m.

DENNY'S PROFESSIONAL CLEANERS
1205 S. Mattis Ave. and 403 W. Kirby Ave.
Phone: (217) 352-1576 and (217) 367-5056
Hours: Daily, 7 a.m. – 11 p.m.

GARBER'S CLEANERS
615 S. Wright St.
Phone: (217) 356-1355
Hours: Monday–Friday, 7:30 a.m. – 5:30 p.m.

PERSONAL TOUCH LAUNDROMAT
104 E. Stoughton St.
Phone: (217) 355-6737.
Hours: Monday–Friday, 8 a.m. – 5 p.m.

STARCREST CLEANERS
202 S. Country Fair Dr.
Phone: (217) 355-8284
Hours: Daily, 7 a.m. – 9 p.m.
1135 Windsor Road
Phone: (217) 355-3415
Hours: Monday–Saturday, 6:30 a.m. – 8:30 p.m. &
Sunday, 10 a.m. – 6 p.m.
611 S. Neil St.
Phone: (217) 352-4801
Hours: Daily, 7 a.m. – 9 p.m.

◉ TAILORS

While some of the dry cleaning facilities listed previously (such as Garber's Cleaners and Country Squire Cleaners) provide clothing services, such as alterations and repairs, there are also a few businesses in town that only do alterations and tailoring. Visit them if you need to look your best for a career fair or formal event.

ANNA'S TAILORING AND ALTERATIONS
1401 N. Prospect Ave.
Phone: (217) 355-9425
Hours: Monday–Friday, 8 a.m. – 6 p.m. &
Saturday, 10 a.m. – 2 p.m.

BARBARA'S ALTERATIONS PLUS
219 S. Locust St.
Phone: (217) 359-2827
Hours: Monday–Friday, 8:30 a.m. – 5 p.m. &
Saturday, 8:30 a.m. – noon

SUKKI'S ALTERATIONS
311 E. Green St.
Phone: (217) 344-1215
Hours: Tuesday–Friday, 10 a.m. – 6 p.m. &
Saturday, 10 a.m. – 4 p.m.

SHOE REPAIR

Unfortunately, none of the shoe repair businesses in the Champaign-Urbana area are located particularly close to campus. However, with a car or via public transportation, there are many options available.
Heel to Toe not only has a repair center but also specializes in custom fittings through quality footwear companies like Birkenstock.

HEEL TO TOE
106 W. Main St.
Phone: (217) 367-2880
Hours: Monday–Thursday, 9:30 a.m. - 5:30 p.m.;
Friday, 9:30 a.m. - 7 p.m.; & Saturday, 9:30 a.m. - 5 p.m.

JJ'S LUGGAGE AND SHOE REPAIR
109 S. Walnut St.
Phone: (217) 352-0111
Hours: Monday–Friday, 8:30 a.m. - 5 p.m. &
Saturday, 10 a.m. - 2 p.m.

MIKHAIL'S SHOE & LUGGAGE REPAIR
1809 Philo Rd.
Phone: (217) 328-7636
Hours: Monday–Friday, 8:30 a.m. - 6 p.m.

LOCAL SERVICES

HAIR AND NAIL SALONS

After a rough week, maybe getting your nails done or getting a sharp new 'do is all it takes to turn it around. Also, you don't want to look unkempt for recruiters or when you entertain visitors. All of these places are equally good, and many are owned by the same firms.

APPEARANCES
512 E. John St.
Phone: (217) 344-4949
Hours: Monday–Friday, 9 a.m. - 5 p.m.

DAZZLING NAILS
45 E. Green St.
Phone: (217) 328-2650
Hours: Monday–Friday, 10 a.m. - 8 p.m.;
Saturday, 10 a.m. - 6 p.m.; & Sunday, noon - 5 p.m.

HAIR BENDERS
703 S. Sixth St
Phone: (217) 384-5050
Hours: Monday–Friday, 9 a.m. - 5 p.m. & Saturday, 11 a.m. - 5 p.m.

LANDO PLACE
707 S. Sixth St.
Phone: (217) 344-0097
Hours: Monday–Friday, 8 a.m. - 6 p.m.

PRETTY NAILS SPA
114 N. Vine St.
Phone: (217) 328-3785
Hours: Monday–Friday, 10 a.m. - 7 p.m.

BARBERS

For those of you looking for an old-fashioned barber shop, C-U has plenty of them to fit your needs, many right on campus. First-time cuts are cheaper, so shop around until you find a barber you like.

DAVE & GENE'S BARBER SHOP
509 E. Green St.
Phone: (217) 367-3797

GLEN'S BARBER SHOP
602 S. First St.
Phone: (217) 355-6439

ILLINOIS CLIPPERS, INC
803 S. Lincoln Ave.
Phone: (217) 328-2369

TANNING SALONS

The sun may not shine in Champaign, but that doesn't mean you can't. Do away with that snowy paleness at any of the dozens of tanning salons on campus. Many use special UV-blocking lights to eliminate any risk of skin cancer. Classic Tan may be the way to go, if only because there's always one nearby, wherever you are in town.

CAMPUS TAN
49 E. Green St.
Phone: (217) 337-0200
Hours: Monday–Friday, 9 a.m. – 9 p.m.;
Saturday, 10 a.m. – 5 p.m.; &
Sunday, noon – 5 p.m.

CLASSIC TAN
710 S. Goodwin Ave.; 1733 W. Kirby Ave.; 703 S. Neil St.;
and 114 N. Vine St.
Phone: (217) 344-6840; (217) 352-7221; (217) 351-2675;
and (217) 367-3707
Hours: Monday–Friday, 9 a.m. – 6 p.m. &
weekends, noon – 5 p.m.

ELECTRIC BEACH TANNING
313 E. Green St.
Phone: (217) 328-4428
Hours: Monday–Friday, 9 a.m. – 9 p.m. &
weekends, 10 a.m. – 9 p.m.

◉ POST OFFICES

US POST OFFICES
302 E. Green St.; 1409 W. Green St.; and 600 N. Neil St.
Phone: (800) ASK-USPS

◉ SHIPPING SERVICES

FEDEX KINKO'S
613 S. Wright St. and 505 S. Mattis Ave.
Phones: (217) 344-2085 and (217) 355-3400
Hours: Monday–Friday, 7 a.m. – 10 p.m. & weekends,
9 a.m. – 5 p.m.; Mattis open 24 hours

UPS STORE
907 W. Marketview Dr.
Phone: (217) 359-6233
Hours: Monday–Friday, 8:30 a.m. – 6:30 p.m. &
Saturday, 9 a.m. – 3 p.m.
1717 W. Kirby Ave.
Phone: (217) 359-4000
Hours: Monday–Friday, 8:30 a.m. – 6:30 p.m. &
Saturday, 9 a.m. – 5 p.m.

◉ CAR SERVICES

Whether you're looking for an oil change, serious maintenance work,
or a shiny new coat of wax, choices abound. Service varies, but
sticking with brand names is probably best because they can ship in
parts faster and more economically.

JIFFY LUBE
201 S. Neil St.
Phone: (217-351-4116)

MIDAS AUTO SERVICE EXPERTS
304 W. University Ave.
Phone: (217-367-0300)

SPEED LUBE OIL CHANGE

307 E. University Ave. and 901 W. Springfield Ave.
Phone: (217) 352-8353 and (217) 355-6682
Hours: Monday–Friday, 8 a.m. – 6 p.m. &
Saturday, 8 a.m. – 5 p.m.

AAMCO TRANSMISSIONS INC.

709 W. Marketview Dr.
Phone: (217) 352-5960
Hours: Monday–Friday, 7:30 a.m. – 5:30 p.m. &
Saturday, 8 a.m. – noon

BILL SMITH AUTO PARTS

3405 N. Countryview Rd.
Phone: (217) 367-5090
Hours: Monday–Friday, 8 a.m. – 5 p.m.

MEINEKE CAR CARE CENTER

712 N. Cunningham Ave.
Phone: (217) 337-1122
Hours: Monday–Saturday, 7:30 a.m. – 6 p.m.

AUTO BATH SYSTEMS

2208 W. Springfield Ave.; 304 Country Fair Dr.;
and 306 E. University Ave.
Phone: (217) 351-3000
Hours: Self-service car wash is open 24 hours a day.

MARKETVIEW CAR WASH

501 W. Marketview Drive
Phone: (217) 355-3065
Hours: Monday–Saturday, 8 a.m. – 6 p.m. &
Sunday, 10 a.m. – 5 p.m.

TRIPLE T CAR WASH, LUBE & DETAIL

1905 W. Bradley Ave.
Phone: (217) 352-9200
Hours: Monday–Friday, 8 a.m. – 5:30 p.m. &
Saturday, 8 a.m. – 5 p.m.

◉ FLORISTS

Surprise the apple of your eye with fresh-cut flowers or just buy some for yourself to celebrate the start of spring or the end of fall. If money is no object, visit Rick Orr in Champaign for superior assembly and long-lasting blooms.

APRIL'S COUNTRY FLORIST
502 E. John St.
Phone: (217) 328-0038
Hours: Monday–Friday,
9 a.m. - 5:30 p.m.

ENGLISH HEDGEROW
406 N. Lincoln Ave.
Phone: (217) 365-0055
Hours: Monday–Saturday,
9 a.m. - 5:30 p.m.

CAMPUS FLORIST
609 E. Green St.
Phone: (217) 344-0051
Hours: Monday–Friday,
9 a.m. - 5 p.m. &
Saturday,
9 a.m. - 5 p.m.

RICK ORR FLORIST
122 N. Walnut St.
Phone: (217) 351-9299
Hours: Monday–Friday,
9 a.m. - 5:30 p.m. &
Saturday,
9 a.m. - 3 p.m.

◉ CARD STORES

Birthdays happen. So do anniversaries. If you're too busy to buy a thoughtful gift, don't be the guy or gal who only leaves a half-hearted wall post. A cheap card will say that you thought about the person at least a little bit in advance.

HALLMARK
119 Lincoln Sq. (Lincoln Square Mall)
Phone: (217) 328-2843
Hours: Monday–Friday, 10 a.m. - 8 p.m. &
Saturday, 10 a.m. - 6 p.m.

113 N. Mattis Ave.
Phone: (217) 355-9119
Hours: Monday–Saturday, 10 a.m. - 8 p.m. &
Saturday, 10 a.m. - 5 p.m.

27 E. Marketview Dr.
Phone: (217) 359-2634
Hours: Monday–Friday, 10 a.m. - 8 p.m.
Saturday, 10 a.m. - 6 p.m. & Sunday, noon - 5 p.m.

COMPUTER REPAIR

All of these providers know what they're doing and can fix most any problem within hours, if not minutes. But call the customer support number of your computer company first; they are probably even more familiar with your machine's issues than these experts and might service it free of charge or for next to nothing.

BEST BUY
2117 N. Prospect Ave.
Phone: (217) 352-8883
Hours: Monday–Saturday, 10 a.m. - 10 p.m. &
Sunday, 11 a.m. - 8 p.m.

LOCAL SERVICES

C-U COMPUTING
802 N. Neil St.
Phone: (217) 239-5022
Hours: Monday–Friday, 8:30 a.m. - 5:30 p.m.

SIMPLIFIED COMPUTERS
901 S. Neil St. #A
Phone: (217) 352-5000
Hours: Monday–Friday, 10 a.m. - 6 p.m. &
Saturday, 10 a.m. - 4 p.m.

CELL PHONE SERVICES

If your phone breaks or you're just looking for the newest style, check out the Champaign Telephone Company. The service is unbeatable, and there are many brands to choose from.

CHAMPAIGN TELEPHONE COMPANY
1300 S. Neil St.
Phone: (217) 359-4282
Hours: Monday–Friday, 8 a.m. - 6 p.m. &
Saturday, 9 a.m. - 4 p.m.

TELXTRA STORE
1976 Roundbarn Rd.
Phone: (217) 355-3595
Hours: Monday–Friday, 9:30 a.m. - 6 p.m. &
Saturday by appointment

VERIZON WIRELESS
910 W. Town Center Blvd.
Phone: (217) 355-0942
Hours: Monday–Saturday, 9 a.m. - 8 p.m. &
Sunday, 11 a.m. - 6 p.m.

◉ GOVERNMENT SERVICES

DEPARTMENT OF MOTOR VEHICLES
2401 W. Bradley Ave.
Phone: (217) 278-3344
Hours: Tuesday, 8 a.m. - 6 p.m.
Wednesday–Friday, 8 a.m. - 5 p.m. &
Saturday, 8 a.m. - noon. Closed Sunday & Monday.

Road tests are offered until an hour before closing on Tuesday and a half hour before closing Wednesday-Saturday.

SOCIAL SECURITY OFFICE
101 S. Country Fair Dr.
Phone: (217) 398-5399
Hours: Monday–Friday, 9 a.m. - 4 p.m.

CHAMPAIGN COUNTY CLERK'S OFFICE (VOTER REGISTRATION)
1776 E. Washington St.
Phone: (217) 384-3720
Hours: Monday–Friday, 8 a.m. - 4:30 p.m.

◉ GOING HOME

Champaign-Urbana's Willard Airport is located at 11 Airport Road (off South Neil Street) in Savoy. It can be reached at (217) 244-8600. C-U MTD's 27 Air Bus runs hourly between 6 a.m. and 7 p.m. during the school year from Green Street across from the Illini Union and Wright Street by the Illini Union Bookstore. It may be easier to fly out of a larger airport in Chicago, Bloomington, or Indianapolis.

If you want to save money, Lincolnland Express (LEX) shuttle service (www.lincolnlandexpress.com), a University of Illinois–approved carrier, provides regularly scheduled trips between various campus locations, including FAR/PAR and Allen Hall, and the Bloomington, Midway, and O'Hare airports. It is advisable to book well in advance when using the LEX service. It is possible to either book online at the above address or by calling (217) 352-6682.

The Suburban Express also provides shuttle service between the University of Illinois campus (including locations at Altgeld Hall and the Armory) and the Chicago airports. Just as with LEX, it is important to book well in advance and to confirm your reservation. Reservations can be made at www.illinishuttle.com or by calling (217) 344-6700. Suburban Express is located at 714 South Sixth Street in Champaign.

"If you're planning on flying out of Midway or O'Hare and you're taking LEX, make sure to book way before you plan on going to make sure you're good to go."

– JEFF, Senior

NUMBERS TO HAVE ON SPEED DIAL

University Police Department
(nonemergency line): **(217) 333-2337**

United States Post Office: **(800) ASK-USPS**

⑤ WHERE TO EAT
AND WHERE TO MEET

As a freshman, you will be required to purchase a meal plan as long as you live in the residence halls. Most plans won't cover all meals, and you'll likely want to eat out throughout the year. Start out with the wide selection on Green Street, Campustown's main thoroughfare. Listed here are primarily the local favorites, the not-too-well-hidden secrets that locals know and love. And if you begin to miss home, many popular franchises are here, too. To get a break from campus altogether, downtown Champaign offers everything from all-night diners to truly fine dining.

⦿ MEAL PLANS

While living in the residence halls, students are required to purchase a meal plan. A lot of flexibility comes with university meal plans because they can be used at any dining hall on campus. Most dining halls include hot meals, sandwich fixings, a salad bar, soda fountains, and dessert. Recently, specialty dining options have been added, ranging from ethnic and regional tastes to vegetarian and kosher selections.

Meal plans are broken up into Classic meals (all-you-can-eat) and Café Credits, i-card credits used to purchase only what students want at A La Carte locations, also known as "Late Night" because many locations serve until midnight.

WHERE TO EAT

CLASSIC MEAL PLANS
14 Classic meals a week
20 Classic meals a week
6 Classic meals a week (graduate hall residents and off-campus students only)

CAFÉ CREDIT PLANS
12 Classic/1,500 Café Credits a week
10 Classic/4,500 Café Credits a week
10 Classic/6,000 Café Credits a week
All Café Credits (11,500) a week

Café Credits are available in varying amounts with Classic meal plans. Although customization is the main appeal of this option, it does have its pitfall—price. Students pay only for what they eat, but they pay full price instead of getting an all-you-can-eat Classic meal. Each Café Credit is approximately worth a penny and is stored on a student's i-card. Although Café Credits give students a lot of flexibility in customizing both their foods and eating times, keeping track of credits involves careful planning.

To add extra credits (Classic or Café) to your i-card, log on to www.housing.uiuc.edu/ncmp/default.aspx. Any currently enrolled university student with an i-card may purchase dining hall credits.

For specific information regarding the dining hall and A La Carte locations near your residence hall, check out http://housing.uiuc.edu/dining. For weekly menus at university dining locations, visit www.housing.uiuc.edu/dining/menus.

TOP ON-CAMPUS DINING OPTIONS

GYROS

Not only is **Zorba's** an Illini tradition, it serves great, fast, inexpensive Greek food. If Zorba's is packed, Niro's Gyros is also good. Both beef and chicken gyros are very tasty. Note the daily specials when you walk in the door.

627 E. Green St.

Phone: (217) 344-0710

Hours: Monday–Wednesday, 10 a.m. - 10 p.m.
Thursday, 10 a.m. - 12:30 a.m.
Friday & Saturday, 11 a.m. - 11 p.m.
Sunday, 11 a.m. - 10 p.m.

PIZZA

Papa Del's serves up the good life to deep-dish lovers. It certainly is the best pizza on campus. Nearby is the row of Papa John's, Domino's, and locally owned Garcia's Pizza. Pizza Hut and Antonio's Pizza, which serves a wide variety by the slice, are located just east of Papa Del's on Green Street.

206 E. Green St.

Phone: (217) 359-7700

Hours: Monday–Thursday, 11:30 a.m. - midnight
Friday & Saturday, 10:30 a.m. - 1:30 a.m.

ON THE GO

A growing fast-food chain, **Za's** offers choose-your-own-ingredients pizzas, pasta, and paninis. Service is fast, and the atmosphere is good. Za's has ample seating for large parties and makes a great study spot.

629 E. Green St.

Phone: (217) 352-2697

Hours: Monday–Friday, 9 a.m. - 9 p.m.
Saturday & Sunday, 11:30 a.m. - 9 p.m.

DINER

With its distinctive smell, **Merry Ann's Diner** is a scene right out of a classic movie. Its hangover menu will wake you up in no time and alleviate any symptoms those late nights may have produced.

1510 S. Neil St.

Phone: (217) 352-5399

Hours: 24 hours a day

◉ OFF-CAMPUS DINING

While Campustown and university dining plans are enough to live off of, stealing away to unfamiliar ground won't leave you hungry. In fact, many of the most delicious yet seldom known plates are off campus, only a short bus ride away. Just as Green Street comes alive at night, so does the open-air seating of downtown Champaign. Whatever your tastes and feelings after being cooped up on campus, metropolitan C-U can satisfy you.

◉ BEST OVERALL

RADIO MARIA

Known for its hip atmosphere, Radio Maria also serves a widely varied and eclectic menu of tapas and entrées.

>119 N Walnut St.
>Phone: (217) 398-7729
>Hours: Monday–Saturday, 11:30 a.m. – 2 a.m.
>   Sunday, 10:30 a.m. – 2 a.m.

KOFUSION

KoFusion is a cultural melting pot that features organic meats and fish. It has a commitment to fine dining in a trendy atmosphere.

>1 E. Main St.
>Phone: (217) 531-1166
>Hours: Lunch: Tuesday–Friday, 11 a.m. – 2 p.m.
>   Dinner: Monday–Friday, 5 p.m. – 11 p.m.
>   Saturday, 3 p.m.- 11 p.m.
>   Sunday, 4 p.m. – 11 p.m.

BACARO

A really fine atmosphere with great seafood, steaks, and pasta.

>113 N. Walnut St.
>Phone: (217) 398-6982
>Hours: Thursday–Sunday, 5 p.m. – 11 p.m.

◉ BEST DATE RESTAURANTS

THE BREAD COMPANY

The Bread Company is a campus gem. It provides an enjoyable and casual setting in a romantic café atmosphere. Order the specialty fondue or choose from pasta and specialty pizzas. It is also open for lunch, serving salads and sandwiches.

706 S. Goodwin Ave.
Phone: (217) 383-1007
Hours: 8 a.m. - 9 p.m.

BACARO

This is simply the most elegant restaurant Champaign-Urbana has to offer. A cozy Italian restaurant located in downtown Champaign, this sophisticated choice will impress any date.

113 N. Walnut St.
Phone: (217) 398-6982
Hours: Thursday–Sunday, 5 p.m. - 11 p.m.

KOFUSION

As the name suggests, KoFusion is fine dining that provides an eclectic mix of foods inspired by Italian, French, American, and Japanese dishes. It will suit those with an adventurous palate who are looking for a sleek, modern atmosphere. Also serves lunch.

1 E. Main St.
Phone: (217) 531-1166
Hours: Lunch: Tuesday–Friday, 11 a.m. - 2 p.m.
Dinner: Monday–Friday, 5 p.m. - 11 p.m.
Saturday, 3 p.m. - 11 p.m.
Sunday, 4 p.m. - 11 p.m.

MIKO RESTAURANT

Teppanyaki chefs, preparing food right before your eyes, are sure to dazzle your loved one. Prices run high, but the complete palette of miso soup, salad, fried rice, and meats make it all worth it.

407 W. University Ave.
Phone: (217) 367-0822
Hours: Monday, 5 p.m. - 10 p.m.
Tuesday–Friday, 11 a.m. - 2 p.m. & 5 p.m. - 10 p.m.
Saturday, 11:30 a.m. - 10 p.m.
Sunday, 11:30 a.m. - 9 p.m.

BEST PLACES TO TAKE YOUR PARENTS

KAMAKURA

A great experience in Japanese cuisine to share with your folks. A wide variety of dishes, including sushi, steak, and tempura, are available. It won't put too much strain on your parents' wallets, either. It's a fun atmosphere for eating good authentic Japanese food.

715 S. Neil St.
Phone: (217) 351-9898
Hours: Monday–Thursday, 11:30 a.m. - 2 p.m. &
5 p.m. - 9:30 p.m.
Saturday & Sunday, noon - 10 p.m.

KENNEDY'S AT STONE CREEK

Perfect if your parents like the country club atmosphere, this restaurant overlooks a golf course. You'll find traditional American fine dining, including a selection of steaks, seafood, and pasta.

2560 Stone Creek Blvd.
Phone: (217) 384-8111
Hours: Lunch: Monday–Thursday, 10 a.m. - 4 p.m.
Friday & Saturday, 10 a.m. - 4 p.m.
Dinner: Monday–Thursday, 4 p.m. - 9 p.m.
Friday & Saturday, 4 p.m. - 10 p.m.
Sunday: Brunch: 11 a.m. - 1:30 p.m.
Lunch: 11 a.m. - 4 p.m.
Dinner: 4 p.m. - 8 p.m.

ALEXANDER'S STEAK HOUSE

Primarily a cook-your-own steakhouse, Alexander's offers the biggest and best steaks in town! All entrees come with all you can eat salad bar, baked potato, and texas toast. Alexander's is wallet friendly and offers a 'student special' year round. Fun for the whole family!

202 W. Anthony Drive
Phone: (217) 359-1789
Hours: Sunday–Thursday, 4 p.m. - 9 p.m.
Friday & Saturday, 4 p.m. - 10 p.m.

WHERE TO EAT

☀ BEST LATE-NIGHT EATS

LA BAMBA

Located in the heart of Campustown, La Bamba is eat-in or take-out Mexican food, and it stays open late. Order all of your Mexican favorites like burritos, tacos, and quesadillas.

606 S. Sixth St.
Phone: (217) 344-6600
Hours: Daily, 11 a.m. – 3 a.m.

MERRY ANN'S DINER

Merry Ann's is Champaign-Urbana's signature 24-hour diner. Enjoy all diner favorites, including breakfast, burgers, and shakes, served around the clock. Perfect for night owls who enjoy the diner atmosphere.

1510 S. Neil St.
Phone: (217) 352-5399
Hours: 24 hours a day

BONNIE JEAN'S

Open till 2 a.m. weekdays and 3 a.m. on weekends, Bonnie Jean's offers pizza, calzones, and sandwiches. Everything is inexpensive and made-to-order. Remember it during those late-night study sessions.

901 S. Fourth St.
Phone: (217) 239-2001
Hours: Sunday–Thursday, 11 a.m. – 2 a.m.
       Friday & Saturday, 11 a.m. – 3 a.m.

INSOMNIA COOKIES

If you're unlucky enough to have late-night cravings and a sweet tooth, you're lucky to have Insomnia Cookies. Buy your cookies and milk here as late as 2:30 in the morning.

502 E. John St.
Phone: (217) 328-0203
Hours: Daily, 4:30 p.m. – 2:30 a.m.

BEST BREAKFAST/BRUNCH

CRÊPE CAFÉ

Crêpe Café offers that thin little French bread and a number of other breakfast foods. Located on Green Street on campus, this unique eatery also serves gelato.

313 E. Green St. # 5
Phone: (217) 344-8575
Hours: Monday–Saturday, 10 a.m. – 10 p.m.
Sunday, 10 a.m. – 3 p.m.

ORIGINAL PANCAKE HOUSE

Head west on Springfield Avenue until you reach the Original Pancake House where you and your friends can enjoy a full breakfast. As it's become known in Champaign and well beyond, this is a fine specialty restaurant to try. It takes a while, and the waiting room is far too small, but it is definitely an upgrade over 24-hour IHOP.

1909 W. Springfield Ave.
Phone: (217) 352-8866
Hours: Wednesday–Sunday, 7 a.m. – 3 p.m.

LE PEEP

Le Peep is another great place to enjoy breakfast or brunch. It also has a great reputation for fine morning dining. This is one of the better Le Peep franchises, so make sure to get there early.

2209 S Neil St.
Phone: (217) 352-7599
Hours: Monday–Friday, 6:30 a.m. – 2:30 p.m.
Saturday & Sunday, 7 a.m. – 2:30 p.m.

WHERE TO EAT

⦿ BEST BURGERS

JUNIOR'S

Junior's specializes in good, inexpensive American food. Grab a burger, fries and shake for just around $5. Great location to grab and go, to or from class.

> 502 E. John St.
> Phone: (217) 337-5577
> Hours: Daily, 11 a.m. - 10 p.m.

ROCK'S

This is a great place to get a burger and enjoy yourself with your friends. Just West of campus.

> 25 E. Springfield Ave.
> Phone: (217) 359-2660
> Hours: Monday–Friday, 11 a.m. - 2 a.m.
> Saturday & Sunday, 6 a.m. - 2 a.m.

JILLIAN'S

Jillian's offers billiards, arcades, and a lot of good American food. Located just West of campus.

> 1201 S. Neil St.
> Phone: (217) 355-2800
> Hours: Sunday–Thursday, 11:30 a.m. - midnight
> Friday & Saturday, 11:30 a.m. - 1 a.m.

⦿ BEST SANDWICHES/SALADS

STRAWBERRY FIELDS CAFÉ

Annexed to the Strawberry Fields grocery store, the café offers vegetarian and health foods. Enjoy sandwiches, pasta salads, and fresh fruit. Located East of campus in Urbana.

> 306 W. Springfield Ave.
> Phone: (217) 328-1655
> Hours: Monday–Saturday, 7 a.m. - 8 p.m.
> Sunday, 10 a.m. - 6 p.m.

JIMMY JOHN'S

This ever-growing sandwich chain, based in Champaign, is popular for a reason. The sandwiches are cheap, fast and delicious. Sit in and eat or take on the go when you're in a hurry. Stays open late and delivers.

43 E. Green St.
Phone: (217) 344-6200
Hours: Monday–Sunday, 11 a.m. – 3 a.m.

PEKARA BAKERY AND BISTRO

Pekara provides great food in a café setting. You will find sandwiches and salads as well as crepes, bakery items, and good coffee and tea.

116 N. Neil St.
Phone: (217) 359-4500
Hours: Daily, 7 a.m. – 10 p.m.

BEST PIZZA

PAPA DEL'S

Easily the best pizza in town and a must-eat for every U of I student. Call in your order early for a deep-dish pizza; there's usually an hour wait.

206 E. Green St.
Phone: (217) 359-7700
Hours: Monday–Thursday, 11:30 a.m. – midnight
Friday & Saturday, 10:30 a.m. – 1:30 a.m.

ANTONIO'S PIZZA

The service is good at this by-the-slice pizzeria that specializes in a variety of creative pizza toppings. Pick up one of their large slices at a good price on the way to class.

619 E. Green St.
Phone: (217) 365-9500
Hours: Sunday, 10:30 a.m. – 8:45 p.m.
Monday, 10:30 a.m. – 11:45 p.m.
Tuesday-Thursday, 10:30 a.m. – 2:45 a.m.

ONE WORLD PIZZA

With a great location in the heart of campus on Green Street, One World is great for takeout or delivery. For those late nights on the town, it's particularly good and cheap.

508 E. Green St.
Phone: (217) 344-4000
Hours: Daily, 11 a.m. – 2:30 a.m.

◉ BEST ITALIAN

ZA'S

One of the better eateries on campus, Za's bridges the gap between inexpensive fast food and premiere Italian cooking. Choose from specialty paninis, pasta, and thin-crust pizza or create your own out of a selection of ingredients. It's somewhat self-service but offers a nice eat-in setting.

> 629 E. Green St.
> Phone: (217) 352-2697
> Hours: Monday–Friday, 9 a.m. – 9 p.m.
>   Saturday & Sunday, 11:30 a.m. – 9 p.m.

BIAGGI'S

Fine Italian dining at medium-range prices located on Neil Street in Champaign. A nice big dining room with fireplaces makes for a good date location.

> 2235 S. Neil St.
> Phone: (217) 356-4300
> Hours: Monday–Thursday, 11 a.m. – 10 p.m.
>   Friday & Saturday, 11 a.m. – 11 p.m.
>   Sunday, 11 a.m. – 9 p.m.

BEST ASIAN

BASIL THAI

Good Thai food in central Campustown? You bet. Check out the food here. Service and location are OK, but the biggest attraction to Basil Thai is the exotic taste of a good coconut, peanut, or curry sauce.

410 E. Green St.
Phone: (217) 344-9130
Hours: Daily, 11 a.m. – 9:30 p.m.

MANDARIN WOK

Mandarin Wok is the best takeout in town and arguably the best place overall given that its clientele is mostly Chinese. Enjoy the typical options and all other Chinese favorites. Inquire about the Chinese menu that includes hundreds more.

403 E. Green St.
Phone: (217) 337-1200
Hours: Tuesday–Sunday, 11:30 a.m. – 3 p.m. & 4:30 p.m. – 9 p.m.
Closed Mondays

WHERE TO EAT

PEKING GARDEN

Located on the edge of downtown Champaign, this is a nice atmosphere to sit and enjoy Chinese food. Peking Garden serves a full array of Chinese dishes.

206 N. Randolph St. # 1
Phone: (217) 355-8888
Hours: Monday–Saturday, 11 a.m. – 10 p.m. (lunch, 11 a.m. – 2 p.m.)
Sunday, noon – 10 p.m.

LAI LAI CHINESE RESTAURANT

Although it appears to be just another Chinese takeout restaurant, Lai Lai offers amazing Chinese food on campus. In addition, the service is always friendly and helpful, and the prices are good.

402 E. Green St.
Phone: (217) 328-1888
Hours: 11 a.m. – 10 p.m.

BEST MEXICAN

DOS REALES

Easily the best Mexican food in town, Dos Reales is truly authentic Mexican cuisine. Service is great, and the location is just north of the engineering campus on University Avenue.

> 1106 W. University Ave.
> Phone: (217) 328-0411
> Hours: Daily, 11 a.m. – 10 p.m.

EL TORO

El Toro is another local authentic Mexican favorite. If this location doesn't suit you, El Toro can be found all over the Champaign-Urbana area, albeit not on campus.

> 1805 S. Neil St.
> Phone: (217) 378-7807
> Hours: Monday–Thursday, 11:30 a.m. – 9:30 p.m.
> Friday & Saturday, 11:30 a.m. – 10 p.m.
> Sunday, 11:30 a.m. – 9 p.m.

LA BAMBA

La Bamba has late hours and is perfect for takeout. Prices are good, and the burritos are allegedly as large as your head.

> 606 S. Sixth St.
> Phone: (217) 344-6600
> Hours: Daily, 11 a.m. – 3 a.m.

"Experience the magic that is La Bamba at 2 a.m. The burritos aren't as big as your head, but they're close."

– NICK, Senior

BEST HEALTH, VEGAN, AND VEGGIE

PASHA MEDITERRANEAN CUISINE

Pasha is located in southwestern Champaign. New to the community, it is quickly becoming known as one of the best places to eat in town. Try many imported and eclectic dishes.

> 2506 Village Green Pl.
> Phone: (217) 355-2200
> Hours: Sunday–Thursday, 11 a.m. – 9 p.m.
>   Friday & Saturday, 11 a.m. – 10:30 p.m.

SAM'S CAFÉ

Sam's has inexpensive food, including breakfast around the clock, and a surprising mix of American and Middle-Eastern dishes.

> 115 N. Walnut St.
> Phone: (217) 352-7102
> Hours: Daily, 9 a.m. – 4 p.m.

RED HERRING

Although hours are a little odd, Red Herring has a communal atmosphere for those looking for a good vegetarian meal. This place is known for preparing vegetarian meals and meals to fulfill various religious requirements.

> 1209 W. Oregon St.
> Phone: (217) 367-2340
> Hours: Breakfast: Monday–Friday, 8:30 a.m. – 11:30 a.m.
>   Lunch: Monday–Friday, 11:30 a.m. – 3 p.m.
>   Dinner: Friday, 6:30 p.m. – 9 p.m.

STRAWBERRY FIELDS

Strawberry Fields is one of the few local businesses with regular hours that is fully committed to raw and prepared vegetarian, vegan, and health food. Salads, sandwiches, and ingredients to make your own healthy and organic dishes are available.

> 306 W. Springfield Ave.
> Phone: (217) 328-1655
> Hours: Monday–Saturday, 7 a.m. – 8 p.m.
>   Sunday, 10 a.m. – 6 p.m.

◉ CHEAPEST EATS

NIRO'S GYROS

Niro's has a variety of good Greek and American fast-food choices. A great place to get a lot of fast food for a little money.

> 1007 W. University Ave.
> Phone: (217) 328-6476
> Hours: Daily, 10:30 a.m. – 11 p.m.

EMPIRE CHINESE RESTAURANT

Traditional affordable Chinese food for take out or dine in. Not much in terms of quality is sacrificed despite Empire's discount, student-friendly deals.

> 410 E. Green St.
> Phone: (217) 328-0832
> Hours: 10:30 a.m. – 11 p.m.

EAST AND WEST FAST FOOD

East and West Fast Food has affordable, vegetarian Indian food with good service. Serves a great buffet at lunch time and takeout and delivery are available during all hours.

> 623 E. Green St.
> Phone: (217) 367-3663
> Hours: Monday–Thursday, noon – 10 p.m.
>   Friday & Saturday, noon – 11 p.m.
>   Sunday, noon – 9 p.m.

DREW'S PIZZA

Drew's Pizza serves whole pizzas for as low as $5 for a large. Especially perfect for late-night cravings and to save a few dollars on a whole lot of food.

> 611 E. Green St.
> Phone: (217) 817-0726
> Hours: Daily, 4 p.m. – 12:30 a.m.

BEST COFFEE

CAFÉ KOPI

The best and most original café environment in Champaign, Café Kopi is a mainstay of the downtown Champaign scene. Meet here for a cup of coffee with a friend. Features regular showings of good local artwork and sits among many of the best shops and restaurants in town. Sidewalk seating is available.

109 N. Walnut St.
Phone: (217) 359-4266
Hours: Daily, 7 a.m. - midnight

WHERE TO EAT

CAFFE PARADISO

This is the best café location on campus. It makes a statement with an original environment. Service is good; sidewalk seating is available.

801 S. Lincoln Ave.
Phone: (217) 384-6066
Hours: Daily, 7 a.m. - 11 p.m.

AROMA CAFÉ

Aroma is a fine café in downtown Champaign. Couch seating and a small patio complement the setting. Aroma also serves some food and is another good meeting place for you and your close friends.

118 N. Neil St.
Phone: (217) 356-3200
Hours: Monday-Friday, 7 a.m. - 11 p.m.
　　　　Saturday & Sunday, 8 a.m. - 11 p.m.

BEST ICE CREAM

JARLING'S CUSTARD CUP

Located just west of campus, Jarling's Custard Cup is a seasonal ice cream shop and local favorite. It's a perfect place to take a date or friends. Try to get some custard here before the warm months melt away.

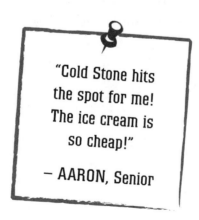

> 309 W. Kirby Ave.
> Phone: (217) 352-2273
> Hours: Monday–Saturday, noon - 10 p.m.
> Sunday, 1 p.m. - 10 p.m.

COZY'S CUSTARD

Good custard offered year-round off campus. Attached to Junior's Burgers.

> 1511 W. Springfield Ave.
> Phone: (217) 355-9020
> Hours: Daily, 11 a.m. - 10 p.m.

COLD STONE CREAMERY

Get serenaded for a pittance at Cold Stone, where it's customary to sing to tipping customers. This is just one of the distinctive qualities of Campustown's only creamery.

> 505 E. Green St.
> Phone: (217) 367-5555
> Hours: Sunday–Thursday, noon - 11 p.m.
> Friday & Saturday, noon - midnight

"Cold Stone hits the spot for me! The ice cream is so cheap!"

– AARON, Senior

BEST PLACES TO WATCH A GAME

ROCK'S

This is a fun place to catch an Illini game if you can't make it to see them in person. Rock's is the place where you can also find your favorite professional sports games and great burgers to eat while watching them.

> 25 E. Springfield Ave.
> Phone: (217) 359-2660
> Hours: Monday-Friday, 11 a.m. – 2 a.m.
> Saturday & Sunday, 6 a.m. – 2 a.m.

BUFFALO WILD WINGS

Known for (you guessed it) buffalo wings, burgers, and the best display of big screens in town, Buffalo Wild Wings is worth the trip for the big game.

> 907 W. Marketview Dr.
> Phone: (217) 378-4400
> Hours: Daily, 11 a.m. – 2 a.m.
> 1335 Savoy Plaza Dr.
> Phone: (217) 356-WING (9464)
> Hours: Daily, 10 a.m. – 2 a.m.

KAM'S

Known nationwide for hosting sports gatherings, Kam's is a place every student must visit at some time. True, it may be crude and dirty at times, but this is a true relic of Campustown. Also buses tailgating fans to home football games.

> 618 E. Daniel St.
> Phone: (217) 328-1605
> Hours: Daily, 10 a.m. – 2 a.m.

JUPITER'S AT THE CROSSING

With three floors of fun, including arcade games and miniature bowling, there's something for everyone. TVs are everywhere so you can watch your favorite team while enjoying their famous pizza, salads, and appetizers.

> 2511 Village Green Place
> Phone: (217) 366-8300
> Hours: Monday - Saturday, 11 a.m. – 2 a.m.
> Sunday, 11 a.m. - 12 a.m.

BEST LOCAL FOOD

EVO CAFÉ

Evo Café is known around campus as the perfect place to pick up a bubble tea—a delicious slushy drink with chewy tapioca balls. This restaurant also serves a variety of Asian food.

711 S. Sixth St.
Phone: (217) 328-7688
Hours: 10:30 a.m. - 10:30 p.m.

LIL PORGY'S

Head east on University Avenue from campus and find truly good barbecue with a distinctive spicy or mild smoked taste. It's really some of the most authentic barbecue around. Enjoy with a lemon shake-up.

101 W. University Ave.
Phone: (217) 367-1018
Hours: Sunday-Thursday, 11 a.m. - 9 p.m.
       Friday & Saturday, 11 a.m. - 10 p.m.

BLUES BBQ

Good barbecue located on campus near the Krannert Center. Found in a nice new setting, Blues features free Wi-Fi.

1103 W. Oregon St.
Phone: (217) 239-9555
Hours: Daily, 11 a.m. - midnight

MOONSTRUCK CHOCOLATE BAR

If you have a taste for gourmet desserts, Moonstruck is the place to be in Champaign-Urbana and is located right next to the Quad on campus. Enjoy a latte with your specialty chocolate or dessert. Take a late-night date or just hang out on the couches and study.

709 S. Wright St.
Phone: (217) 367-7402
Hours: Monday-Friday, 7 a.m. - 11 p.m.
       Saturday & Sunday, 9 a.m. - 11 p.m.

BEST FOOD DELIVERED TO YOUR DORM

CAMPUSFOOD.COM

Many of the restaurants listed here deliver to the residence halls and anywhere in town you may need a bite. Check out www.campusfood.com for a comprehensive list of delivered food items. You can order right there or find numbers to order by phone.

"Not many people do this because of the flexibility of campus dining. Campusfood.com is sometimes pretty slow."

– JANE, Sophomore

NUMBERS TO HAVE ON SPEED DIAL

Insomnia Cookies: **(217) 328-0203**

Bonnie Jean's: **(217) 239-2001**

Jimmy John's: **(217) 344-6200**

Papa Del's: **(217) 359-7700**

One World Pizza: **(217) 344-400**

⑥ RECREATION,
ENTERTAINMENT, AND THE ARTS

As a college town, Champaign-Urbana has a lot to offer. If you're a student who likes music, sports, or the arts, you'll have a lot to choose from (if you can pull yourself away from your studies). In addition to supporting your fellow classmates in the arts or out on the sports field, Champaign-Urbana attracts a lot of world-class talent that comes to play for students like you. In the past, talent as distinctive as Yo-Yo Ma or as popular as Kanye West have visited and entertained.

◉ LIVE MUSIC VENUES

Whatever your preference, live music isn't hard to come by in C-U. Most acts, however, only come through on weekends, which might be preferable anyway because students aren't as busy then.

CANOPY CLUB

Canopy Club is located on campus and attracts many world-class rock and hip-hop musicians. The large setting includes a large standing room area and a few tables on the floor. There is also a balcony where you can relax and watch the show in stadium-style seats. Check around campus during the year for concert updates.

708 S. Goodwin Ave.
Phone: (217) 367-3140
Hours: Daily, 9 p.m. – 2 a.m.

THE IRON POST

Located in downtown Urbana, the Iron Post is a small venue with a local stage that attracts jazz, blues, and rock musicians, primarily from the area. Check postings online or at the venue to discover local talent that may surprise you.

120 S. Race St.
Phone: (217) 337-7678
Hours: Daily, 9 p.m. – 2 a.m.

HIGHDIVE

Downtown Champaign's premiere music venue, the Highdive brings in a number of rock and hip-hop acts. It has a large concert area, including some balcony seating, and a lot of sitting and standing room. There is also outside seating available.

51 E. Main St.
Phone: (217) 356-2337
Hours: Daily, 9 p.m. – 2 a.m.

ASSEMBLY HALL

In addition to being home to Illini Basketball, the Assembly Hall hosts a variety of talents. If an artist is big enough to fill a stadium, they will be found at the Assembly Hall. Tickets for standing room and stadium seating are often available.

1800 S. First St. # 101
Phone: (217) 333-5000

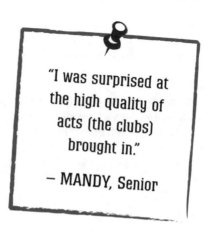

"I was surprised at the high quality of acts (the clubs) brought in."

— MANDY, Senior

⊙ CAMPUS RECREATION CENTER

There are two main campus recreation centers on campus.

CAMPUS RECREATION CENTER-EAST (CRCE)

Campus Recreation Center-East, or "sir-see," is located next to Allen Hall. Although smaller than its western counterpart, it contains a swimming pool with waterslide, spa, indoor soccer arena, 3 basketball/volleyball courts, 3 racquetball courts, a 10,000 square foot area with weight and cardio machines, and a 3-lane track encompassing them all.

INTRAMURAL-PHYSICAL EDUCATION BUILDING (IMPE)

The Intramural-Physical Education Building has traditionally been the main campus recreation center. It has been undergoing renovations that should be unveiled sometime in the spring of 2008. When it reopens, IMPE will feature more than a dozen basketball/volleyball courts, 15 squash/racquetball courts, an indoor and outdoor pool, and a 34,000 square foot weight and fitness room.

Each facility also has multipurpose areas for everything from yoga to dance to combat classes. For more information, log on to www.campusrec.uiuc.edu.

CINEMAS

In addition to those listed below, Champaign-Urbana is also home to the annual Ebertfest, hosted by U of I alumnus and Pulitzer Prize winner Roger Ebert at the immense Virginia Theatre.

BOARDMAN'S ART THEATRE

Boardman's is a recently updated art theatre with fantastic sound, seating, and screen in a classic theater setting. It usually shows one movie continually throughout the week, and running time varies. Still, it's a good place to see foreign and independent films and documentaries.

126 W. Church St.
Phone: (217) 355-0068

SAVOY 16

Located just south of Champaign in Savoy, this is the area's most popular multiplex. See most movies with a national release.

232 Burwash Ave.
Phone: (217) 355-3456

BEVERLY CINEMA 18

Another multiplex located on the far north end of Champaign, this is a very inexpensive place to see a movie. Beverly Cinema offers all of the latest releases with great rates for students.

910 Meijer Dr.
Phone: (217) 359-5687

VIRGINIA THEATRE

Since 1921, this historic landmark has offered entertainment to the masses.

203 W. Park
Phone: (217) 356-9053 (office)
(217) 356-9063 (tickets)

● THE ARTS

Listed here are some of the best places to see theater and performing arts. But check calendars throughout the year to find a hidden world all over campus; many of your daytime classrooms become venues for student, community, national, and international artists throughout the year.

KRANNERT CENTER FOR THE PERFORMING ARTS

The Krannert Center is a great place to see anything from a student-performed play to a master of classical music. Ballet and other fine art performances are scheduled throughout the school year. Pick up a schedule upon arriving.

> 500 S. Goodwin Ave.
> Phone: (217) 333-6280

PARKLAND COLLEGE THEATRE

Parkland College offers a chance to not only see a great play but to act in one. Look for dates for auditions and performances to see great off-campus community theater, featuring students, children, and adults.

> 2400 W. Bradley Ave.
> Phone: (217) 351-2528

● MUSEUMS

SPURLOCK MUSEUM

This university museum is free with a highlight on various ancient cultures and their origins. An interesting and brief tour, including a lot of illuminating information and artifacts, is available daily.

> 600 S. Gregory St.
> Phone: (217) 333-2360

JAPAN HOUSE

An artistic representation of Japanese history located right on the UIUC campus. Regular tours and tea ceremonies are held at this beautiful international portal. Japan House is near the FAR/PAR residence halls.

> 2000 S. Lincoln Ave.
> Phone: (217) 244-9934

⊛ SKATING

UI ICE ARENA
Home of Illini Hockey, the Ice Arena has open skates for students and the community. Skates can be rented very cheaply.

406 E. Armory Ave.
Phone: (217) 333-2081

SKATELAND
If roller skating is your forte, check out Skateland in Savoy. Savoy is located just south of Champaign.

208 W. Curtis Rd., Savoy
Phone: (217) 359-3335.

⊛ BOWLING ALLEYS

Bowling makes great bonding and is less intensive than practically any other sport. With food nearby and a leisurely atmosphere, hitting the lanes can serve as a competitive outlet and a good networking locale.

RECREATION ENTERTAINMENT

ILLINI UNION BOWLING LANES
These lanes hold student specials and are even the place of some recreational courses in kinesiology.

1401 E. Green St. #115
Phone: (217) 333-2415

ARROWHEAD LANES
Weeknight specials include $2 games several days a week.

1401 N. McKinley Ave.
Phone: (217) 352-5288

G.T.'S WESTERN BOWL
G.T.'s has many leagues, both semiprofessional and simply social, to choose from.

917 Francis Dr.
Phone: (217) 359-1678

⊛ GYMS

In case CRCE or IMPE is overcrowded (and they can be), considering a fitness membership might not be a bad idea. Here are some of the better local choices.

CURVES
1808 Round Barn Rd. and 2200 E. University Ave.
Phone: (217) 398-9780 and (217) 365-9444

EVOLVE FITNESS STUDIO
41 E. University Ave.
Phone: (217) 641-3123

GOLD'S GYM
1914 Round Barn Rd. and 1305 E. Colorado Ave.
Phone: (217) 359-3476 and (217) 344-4653

⊛ GOLF COURSES

Hit the links around town and look around the pro shops for the latest clubs, bags, and accessories. Rounds are easy to schedule and clubs can be rented cheaply.

CHAMPAIGN COUNTRY CLUB
1211 S. Prospect Ave.
Phone: (217) 356-1255

LINCOLNSHIRE FIELDS COUNTRY CLUB
2000 Byrnebruk Dr.
Phone: (217) 352-1911

PUTT ZONE FUN CENTER
815 Dennison Dr.
Phone: (217) 356-6121

STONE CREEK GOLF CLUB
2600 Stone Creek Blvd.
Phone: (217) 367-3000

URBANA GOLF & COUNTRY CLUB
100 W. Country Club Rd.
Phone: (217) 367-8449

◉ PARKS

Enjoy the lushness nature affords us before it gets too cold. Have a picnic, plop down on the grass, or find a quiet place to jog. Very few are near campus, so you may be better off just sunning on the Quad, but city parks are usually less crowded and a nice escape on a weekend afternoon with friends.

WEST SIDE PARK
Located just west of downtown Champaign, West Side Park is a fine haven covering about 4 blocks. It has one of the best playgrounds around.

400 W. University Ave.

CRYSTAL LAKE PARK
Located northeast of campus, Crystal Lake Park covers 90 acres. The lake is often used for small boats and fishing. Paddle boat rentals are fairly cheap.

206 W. Park St.

CARLE PARK
Carle Park is located in central Urbana and is walking or biking distance from campus. It is an 8-acre area for meeting and relaxing.

The corner of Indiana and Garfield avenues

◉ DAY TRIPS

CURTIS ORCHARD
Curtis Orchard is an apple and pumpkin farm on the southwest corner of Champaign.

3902 S. Duncan Rd.
Phone: (217) 359-5565

ROBERT ALLERTON PARK
Located about 30 miles west of Champaign near Monticello, this fantastic park is owned by the university. Named one of the "Eight Wonders of Illinois," Allerton Park is a fantastic meeting of garden, nature, architecture, and art. It covers more than 1,500 acres.

515 Old Timber Rd., Piatt County
Phone: (217) 333-3287

HARVEST MOON DRIVE-IN

Although it may seem a stretch to drive 40 minutes to see a movie, many students find it rewarding to experience film in this outdoor country setting.

Route 47, Gibson City, IL

TURKEY RUN STATE PARK

Sure it's a hike by car, and definitely on foot when you get there, but this rare wilderness is built for nature lovers. Hike easy to challenging trails and go canoeing or tubing in the water. Stop by the Beef House on the way back for their famous rolls.

8121 E. Park Rd., Marshall, IN

Phone: (765) 597-2635

CHICAGO

Illinois isn't just farms. Located just two and a half hours north of campus, Chicago is a world-class city that offers just about everything a student could want. Although you won't be able to experience even close to everything in just a day, have a taste of shopping, shows, professional sports, Lake Michigan, and pretty much anything else you may miss in the small town of Champaign-Urbana.

Highlights include the Shedd Aquarium, Navy Pier, and the Art Institute. If the weather's warm, take an afternoon off and see the Cubs or White Sox. Once you get to Chicago, almost every place is accessible through the Chicago Transit Authority (CTA).

ST. LOUIS

About an equal distance from Champaign-Urbana as Chicago, many Chicago natives choose to go here for something different. St. Louis offers shopping, shows, and professional sports teams, and of course the great Gateway Arch.

◉ NOTES

_____

_____

_____

_____

_____

_____

_____

_____

_____

_____

_____

_____

_____

_____

NUMBERS TO HAVE ON SPEED DIAL

Campus Recreation: **(217) 333-3806**

Urbana Park District: **(217) 367-1544**

Allerton Park: **(217) 333-3287**

Curtis Orchard: **(217) 359-5565**

⑦ STOP N SHOP

Champaign-Urbana may not compete with Chicago's Magnificent Mile, but everything you need you can find either in the North Prospect Avenue/Neil Street area or in downtown Champaign. The area features many typical stores at Marketplace Mall, and downtown is the place to go for vintage/resale items. All in all, C-U has an abundance of boutiques for both weekday and weekend consumers, if they know where to look and regardless of their budget constraints.

GROCERY STORES AND PHARMACIES

It's always a good idea to have a few snacks stocked up, so you don't need to go out or order in all the time. Or maybe you have a prescription to refill. Walgreens is the only on-campus grocery. As a result, prices are inflated somewhat, but not ridiculously. Off-campus stores have the type of selection you may be accustomed to.

WALGREENS
407 E. Green St.
Phone: (217) 344-0121

SCHNUCKS
200 N. Vine St.
Phone: (217) 337-6016

COUNTY MARKET
220 N. Broadway Ave.
Phone: (217) 384-3366

AM-KO
Asian specialty store
101 E. Springfield Ave.
Phone: (217) 398-2922

JERRY'S IGA
312 W. Kirby Ave.
Phone: (217) 352-0019

MEIJER
2401 N. Prospect Ave.
Phone: (217) 353-4000

STOP N SHOP

DISCOUNT STORES

Buying in bulk? Or just want the basics? These discount shops have the items you're most likely to need and at low, low prices.

CIRCLE K
1713 W. John St.
Phone: (217) 359-4515

COLONIAL PANTRY FOOD STORE
312 E. Green St.
Phone: (217) 373-8416

COMMON GROUND FOOD CO-OP
403 S. Wright St.
Phone: (217) 352-3347

DOLLAR GENERAL
2004 W. Springfield Ave.
Phone: (217) 351-3013

SAVE-A-LOT
220 N. Broadway Ave.
Phone: (217) 384-6885

DÉCOR FOR THE DORM

Those walls will sure look empty when you move in. Spice up your room with some colorful accessories that reveal all the quirks of your personality (or the ones you want people to know about). Just make sure to not leave lasting marks.

ART MART

With inventory ranging from abstract furniture to designer delicacies, this all-in-one off-campus locale is a true treasure for furnishing your room.

127 Lincoln Square
Phone: (217) 344-7979

BED BATH & BEYOND

This distant store is perfect for filling out your bathroom with everything from basic bedding and sheets to specialty soaps and plush pillows for lounging.

51 E. Marketview Dr.
Phone: (217) 356-8490

TANGER OUTLET CENTER

Don't let the lack of proximity fool you—this place has it all. You will soon appreciate its low prices, immense variety, and pleasing wait staff. It's about 30 minutes on I-57 South; make it a weekend excursion.

D400 Tuscola Blvd., Tuscola, IL.
Phone: (217) 253-2282

TARGET

Target has a good selection of affordable furniture. They have stylish décor that you would normally pay a fortune for.

2102 N Prospect Avenue
Phone: (217) 355-3325

MALLS AND SHOPPING CENTERS

Sometimes a day of shopping is all you need to remind yourself of the enormous suburban malls back home. Get several errands done at once with a quick meal in between, either at a food court or next door.

MARKETPLACE MALL

The area's main mall, it includes a food court and many clothing stores, such as Gap, Abercrombie, American Eagle, Limited, and many others. Several large department stores are attached. This is a typical American mall, featuring the best places to find clothes and shoes in the area.

2000 N. Neil St.

Phone: (217) 356-2700

LINCOLN SQUARE MALL

A somewhat sparse mall with many local establishments, Lincoln Square features most prominently Art Mart, a fine little store for décor and international groceries.

201 Lincoln Square

Phone: (217) 367-4092

OLD FARM SHOPS

This urban shopping center houses a variety of premier boutiques, including Jos. A Bank and Talbot's clothiers and Panera Bread for a midshopping snack.

Corner of Kirby and Mattis avenues

ROUND BARN BANQUET CENTER

Named after the rotund barn it is built around, this miniature mall possesses dry cleaning service, a nail salon, and Famous Dave's BBQ, arguably some of the best barbecue in the twin cities.

1900 Round Barn Rd.

Phone: (217) 359-9800

SUNNYCREST MALL

Although far away from campus (take the 2 Red bus), this mall, located next to a major branch of Busey Bank, has more stand-alone restaurants than the others. American, Chinese, and Mexican cuisine can be found near the County Market and Walgreens.

1717 S. Philo Rd.

Phone: (217) 384-5787

MEN'S AND WOMEN'S CLOTHING

You couldn't bring ALL your clothes down, could you? Or maybe you've grown a few sizes or want to define your style a little better. Either way, a few clothing stores unique to C-U can hook you up or you could take the traditional route with classic outfitters.

PITAYA
One of campus's few clothing shops, Pitaya is a women's clothing store that features a lot of trendy items.
> 625 E. Green St.
> **Phone: (217) 365-6666**

BACHRACH
Located in Marketplace Mall, Bachrach ships in an array of men's professional clothing and business suits. A friendly yet knowledgeable staff does alterations flawlessly and can handle fashion emergencies at a moment's notice.
> 2000 N. Neil St.
> **Phone: (217) 352-3274**

DANDELION
A well-known local store for finding vintage and used clothing, particularly creative items, Dandelion is good for costumes or for resurrecting a funky style.
> 9 E. Taylor St.
> **Phone: (217) 355-9333**

KOHL'S DEPARTMENT STORE
Stocks retail brand-name clothing at discount prices.
> 109 Convenience Center Rd.
> **Phone: (217) 352-0431**

OLD NAVY

Old Navy is a popular men's and women's clothing store for inexpensive necessity clothing items. It is located in the general North Prospect Avenue shopping area.

716 W. Town Center Blvd.
Phone: (217) 398-6403

PLATO'S CLOSET

Plato's Closet sells gently worn brand-name clothing, predominantly gathered from young adults. The prices are very reasonable, and this is a good place to sell the jeans you don't want anymore or to relive a recent fashion trend with clothing that has already been shrunk in the washing machine.

29 E. Marketview Dr.
Phone: (217) 366-8200

"Plato's Closet is a great way to get rid of old clothes without wasting them. They offer pretty good prices for clothes that have gone out of style, at least compared to garage sales."

– JOSE, Sophomore

STOP N SHOP

MUSIC STORES

Miss high school band? Perhaps you took a general education class and found your musical vocation. Shop around the musical menageries to find an instrument that will suit your style. Many used ones are in excellent shape and can hit the high notes with a minimal drain on your budget.

EXILE ON MAIN STREET

Exile on Main Street, named for a famous Rolling Stones album, is local to downtown Champaign. It sells new and used CDs, DVDs, and video games. Buy, sell, trade, and support local entrepreneurs here.

1 E. Main St.
Phone: (217) 398-6246

C.V. LLOYDE MUSIC CENTER

For over 135 years, C.V. Lloyde Music Center has continued to provide the best customer-service around. They specialize in installations, repairs, rentals, and lessons.

102 S. Neil
Phone: (217) 352-7031

CORSON MUSIC

if you are looking for guitar sheet music, this is the place to go. They carry many unique titles. They even have sheet music for the mandolin.

202 W. Main
Phone: (217) 367-3898

THE MUSIC SHOPPE

As its name indicates, this store is all about instruments. With the best variety in town, The Music Shoppe has got you covered with an experienced staff that can help with repairs and sell accessories.

114 S. Neil St.
Phone: (217) 356-8005

⊙ JEWELERS

Ladies, treat yourself to something nice with that gift certificate or check you got from your relatives. Men, some occasions call for a little bling to show you're serious and in a relationship for the long haul.

BROWNE'S FINE JEWELRY

Most items here will be more than a tad out of your price range, but there are several smaller objects you won't have to splurge for to show you care for that special someone.

302 W. Kirby Ave.
Phone: (217) 352-2575

GOLD RUSH II

This unusual store, which doubles as a pawn shop, specializes in musical instruments. A variety of loosely worn chains, necklaces, and earrings are also stocked.

41 E. Main St.
Phone: (217) 355-0010

INTERNATIONAL GALLERIES

This shop collects artsy works from all over the world, encompassing a myriad of aesthetic styles. Prices vary a great deal, but this is not a typical wedding ring jeweler.

300 S. Broadway Ave.
Phone: (217) 328-2254

ZALES: THE DIAMOND STORE

Yes, the famed jewelry vendor has set up shop in commercial C-U. Pieces are generally more expensive than even Browne's, but the cuts are world class and worthy of engagement rings, if you're that far along in your relationship.

2000 N. Neil St. # B16
Phone: (217) 398-5015

GREEK APPAREL AND SPORTING GOODS

Proud of your college or house? Stock up at these places, so no matter where you go, people will know how the university has reinforced your allegiances.

T.I.S. BOOKSTORE

In addition to being a textbook buyer and seller, T.I.S. sells university-brand clothing and customized Greek apparel and merchandise.

707 S. Sixth St.

Phone: (217) 337-4900

TE' SHURT'

Te' shurt' specializes in custom printing. Put in orders for custom apparel or pick up your Greek gear here.

711 S. Wright St.

Phone: (217) 344-1226

GAMEDAY SPIRIT

Probably the best store on campus for UI athletic apparel, Gameday Spirit regularly sells the clothing you need to fit in at the game.

519 E. Green St.

Phone: (217) 328-7722

FOLLETT'S BOOKSTORE

Although smaller than T.I.S., Follett's carries some items that cannot be found anywhere else. It also concentrates on athletic apparel, in addition to selling books in place of Greek clothing.

627 S. Wright St.

Phone: (217) 356-1368

THE QUAD SHOP

Within the Illini Union lies this convenience store/apparel outfitter. What you pick up here is straight from the university itself. The space is used efficiently, but a smaller selection of team gear is available here.

1401 E. Green St.

NEW BOOKS

Everybody loves pristine unopened books. Get them at these university-licensed official retailers that know exactly what books your instructors want. This is the only guaranteed way to get the right things, albeit maybe not at the ideal cost.

ILLINI UNION BOOKSTORE (IUB)

The university's official new and used textbook seller. Pick up your books or try to sell your used books here. IUB is well-organized, and it's easy to find everything here. Profits go toward Registered Student Organizations.

809 S. Wright St.
Phone: (217) 333-2050

FOLLETT'S BOOKSTORE

Although the selection of textbooks isn't as good as T.I.S. or IUB, this is a good place to pick up your books and your other needed school supplies. Follett's also sells a good deal of university merchandise and apparel.

627 S. Wright St.
Phone: (217) 356-1368

STOP N SHOP

T.I.S. BOOKSTORE

T.I.S. sells about half of the textbooks on campus, and some instructors only publish their course manuals/packets through T.I.S. instead of IUB. With a rewards club program, students receive a percentage of their receipts back to spend on handy things like pizza and T-shirts.

707 S. Sixth St.
Phone: (217) 337-4900

⦿ USED BOOKS

On a tight budget? Save money by buying cheap from students who have taken classes before you. Make sure they're the right texts still; an added bonus is that helpful notes or answers are often already written in.

ILLINIBOOKEXCHANGE.COM (IBX)

Highly recommended for anyone who wants to put in the time and energy to save a great deal of money. Textbooks are very expensive and are made even more expensive by bookstores trying to pull a profit. Through the Illini Book Exchange, you can deal directly with students. This way, you can save on your needed textbooks and make more on what you no longer need. It's also smart to talk with your friends about what they're taking at the beginning of each semester, to make sure you can save money by dealing directly with them.

Even with all of the potential savings, make sure to verify that the books you're buying are still acceptable for your courses. The only other downside to IBX is that you have to agree to meet the buyer/seller, often at a public place, however, with its recent partnership with campus bookstores, most exchanges now take place with representatives nearby.

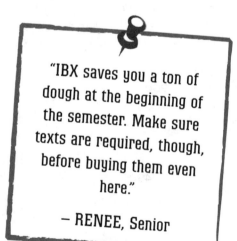

"IBX saves you a ton of dough at the beginning of the semester. Make sure texts are required, though, before buying them even here."

— RENEE, Senior

◉ NOTES

_____

_____

_____

_____

_____

_____

_____

_____

_____

_____

_____

_____

_____

_____

_____

STOP N
SHOP

NUMBERS TO HAVE ON SPEED DIAL

T.I.S. Bookstore: **(217) 337-4900**

Walgreens: **(217) 344-0121**

Marketplace Mall: **(217) 356-2700**

 # BLAH, BLAH,
AND WHATEVER

As a campus, the university offers numerous resources. The university is there not just to help you to learn, but to help you succeed in the same ways that you did at home, as well as to explore new things. When you graduate, most university colleges will help set you on your way to finding a job or to furthering your education.

Whatever your aspirations for down the road, there are some things you need to know so that you'll be better informed. These "things to know" aren't necessarily crucial to your success, but reading some, like legal policies, may make the difference between you checking out of college early and you completing your studies on time without incident. Toward the end of this guide, you'll find some Web sites to add to your bookmarks right away and a few more of the tidbits and anecdotes that make the University of Illinois what it is.

LOCAL HOTELS

When your parents visit (and they probably will want to), they cannot stay in your room. Put them up in a nice hotel near campus or a well-reputed chain where they can commute from. Champaign has many lodging locations, but beware of the low-priced ones. They are that way for a reason, and your parents already spent all that money on gas or airfare, so what's another $50/night? The Union is actually the best place for both hospitality and location, but vacancies are few and far between.

ILLINI UNION GUEST HOTEL
Ideal for those who want a central campus location, parents and visitors can stay right in the Illini Union. It offers most of the amenities of a good, basic hotel with location being the main added bonus. Step out of the room and right onto the Quad.

> 1401 W. Green St.
> Phone: (217) 333-3030

DRURY INN
Drury Inn is definitely one of the nicer hotels available to visitors. Located near I-74 on the north end of Champaign, this is a good modern hotel for Mom and Dad.

> 905 W. Anthony Drive
> Phone: (217) 398-0030

HOLIDAY INN
A good three-star hotel located near campus in Urbana, this is another fine place for a visitor to stay. Visitors won't save too much money here, but they're guaranteed a comfortable rest.

> 1001 Killarney St.
> Phone: (877) 508 1762

◉ VOLUNTEER OPPORTUNITIES

Giving back to the community can be a very rewarding experience and shake up your weekends in a positive way. Nearly every religious institution, Greek organization, or Registered Student Organization aids Champaign-Urbana through some means, so those other interests would be good places to start.

Volunteer Illini Projects is by far the largest RSO devoted solely to volunteerism and has many exciting fundraisers, tutoring programs, city beautification projects, and mentoring programs set up. Chances are someone you have met is in it, so ask them what it's all about if you're curious.

"Seeing the fruits of your labor in action is incredible! People love the help, and the college students' enthusiasm!"

— JANE, Sophomore

LOCAL HOUSES OF WORSHIP

The major religions all have extraordinary facilities on campus and are all undergoing massive additions. For a comprehensive listing of places of worship, visit www.ourchampaign.com/html/main/org/org_catID/4/index.html.

ASSEMBLY OF GOD: CROSSROADS CAMPUS CHURCH
912 W. Springfield Ave.
Phone: (217) 337-1681

BAPTIST: UNIVERSITY BAPTIST CHURCH
314 E. Daniel St.
Phone: (217) 344-0484

BIBLE: TWIN CITY BIBLE CHURCH
806 W. Michigan Ave.
Phone: (217) 344-0641

BUDDHIST: PRAIRIE ZEN CENTER
515 S. Prospect Ave.
Phone: (217) 355-3835

CATHOLIC: ST. JOHN'S CATHOLIC NEWMAN CENTER
604 E. Armory Ave.
Phone: (217) 344-1184

CHARISMATIC: CURTIS ROAD CHURCH OF GOD
2604 W. Curtis Rd.
Phone: (217) 359-8285

CHRISTIAN: FIRST CHRISTIAN CHURCH
3601 S. Staley Rd.
Phone: (217) 356-1649

CHRISTIAN REFORMED: HESSEL PARK CHURCH
700 W. Kirby Ave.
Phone: (217) 356-3177

CHURCH OF CHRIST: PHILO ROAD CHURCH OF CHRIST
2601 S. Philo Rd.
Phone: (217) 344-1659

BLAH, BLAH

CHURCH OF THE NAZARENE: NEW DAY COMMUNITY CHURCH

2611 W. Springfield Ave.
Phone: (217) 356-4747

EPISCOPAL: ST. JOHN THE DIVINE

1011 S. Wright St.
Phone: (217) 344-1924

GREEK ORTHODOX: THREE HIERARCHS GREEK ORTHODOX CHURCH

2010 Three Hierarchs Ct.
Phone: (217) 352-3452

INTERDENOMINATIONAL: COVENANT FELLOWSHIP CHURCH

1203 W. Green St.

ISLAMIC: CENTRAL ILLINOIS MOSQUE AND ISLAMIC CENTER

106 S. Lincoln Ave.
Phone: (217) 344-1555

JEWISH: HILLEL FOUNDATION

503 E. John St.
Phone: (217) 344-1328

LUTHERAN: ST. ANDREW'S CHURCH

909 S. Wright St.
Phone: (217) 344-1593

MENNONITE: FIRST MENNONITE CHURCH

902 W. Springfield Ave.
Phone: (217) 367-5353

PRESBYTERIAN: FIRST PRESBYTERIAN CHURCH

302 W. Church St.
Phone: (217) 356-7238

QUAKER: URBANA-CHAMPAIGN FRIENDS MEETING

PO Box 34, Urbana, IL 61803
Phone: (217) 328-5853

UNITARIAN UNIVERSALIST: UNITARIAN

UNIVERSALIST CHURCH
309 W. Green St.
Phone: (217) 384-8862

UNITED CHURCH OF CHRIST: COMMUNITY UNITED CHURCH OF CHRIST
805 S. Sixth St.
Phone: (217) 344-5091

UNITED METHODIST: WESLEY UNITED METHODIST CHURCH
1203 W. Green St.
Phone: (217) 344-1120

UNITED PENTECOSTAL: APOSTOLIC LIFE, UPC
2107 High Cross Rd.
Phone: (217) 367-5433

THE VINEYARD
1500 N. Lincoln Ave.
Phone: (217) 384-3070

WESLEYAN: FIRST WESLEYAN CHURCH
408 E. Illinois St.
Phone: (217) 367-4566

WORD/FAITH: HARVEST CHURCH
408 E. Illinois St.
Phone: (217) 367-4566

GREEN BUILDINGS

As society learns more about the environment and climate change, the importance of environmentally friendly buildings grows with each passing day. After all, it only makes sense that scientists studying ways to stave off global warming should pollute as little as possible themselves. As a result, the University of Illinois has been a trendsetter in improving designs to reduce carbon footprints and the strain upon local ecosystems.

Beginning with the new Business Instructional Facility, all university construction now meets Leadership in Energy and Environmental Design (LEED) certification criteria with higher levels of accreditation required for larger projects. In other words, minor renovations need only match LEED certification rules, while classroom-housing facilities must take LEED Silver or Gold standards into account during planning.

Besides the university, C-U has consistently placed highly among peer cities for eco-friendliness. Both Urbana and Champaign have been named "Tree City USA" for their continued commitment to planting and caring for trees. The U-CYCLE recycling program in Urbana supplies large bins to all residents, and while Champaign does not have a similar initiative, only a far-off dump site, city officials are working toward making recycling access as efficient as possible.

UNIVERSITY AND LEGAL VIOLATIONS

While these rules may be obvious, knowing the letter of the law as well as the penalties for infractions might keep you from engaging in risky or dangerous behavior. Some policies will seem stricter than high school, but you're an adult now and responsibility, as you have probably been told, increases with age.

ACADEMIC

The university takes plagiarism seriously, and students are constantly reminded of the policy on fair use of others' work. Failure to adhere to this policy has dire consequences with the Student Discipline Committee and may lead to expulsion.

ALCOHOL

The state of Illinois's maximum blood alcohol concentration level for persons 21 and older is .08. There is an open container law prohibiting open alcoholic beverages from being transported in public. One has to be 19 to enter Champaign bars and 18 for Urbana bars. Police will raid bars, so don't get caught with a fake ID. If underage students are within an arm's reach of an alcoholic drink, they may be issued a drinking ticket.

FINES

Underage students in possession of alcohol face a $300 fine in Champaign and $135 in Urbana. If a student is severely intoxicated, he or she will be sent to a hospital via ambulance, costing a minimum of $1,500.

DRIVING

The posted speed limit for most of the university district is 25 mph. According to state law, motorists must always wear seat belts and yield to pedestrians at intersections as well as at a number of midstreet crosswalks stationed across campus. Many Campustown streets are one-way, so be aware when planning turns.

SMOKING

Controlled substances are prohibited in university buildings, and smoking cigarettes is illegal statewide inside all buildings. Possession of drug paraphernalia is also subject to punishment if discovered in the residence halls.

TREATMENT

The Office of Alcohol and Drug Services works with troubled students through counseling and peer-to-peer workshops. Typically students will not be disciplined for a first violation, although in especially severe cases they may.

CAMPUS SLANG

Six Pack-The group of residence halls on the southwest corner of campus.

MTD-Short for Champaign-Urbana Mass Transit District, this generally refers to the buses that run frequently on and off campus.

DI-*The Daily Illini,* UIUC's independent college newspaper.

Late Night-A La Carte locations or areas of student housing where students can purchase food using Café Credits as late as midnight (1 a.m. on weekends).

RSOs-Registered Student Organizations.

Quad Day-A day early in the school year when RSOs gather on the Quad to attract new members.

TAs-Graduate teaching assistants who teach many sections at the university.

UGL-Undergraduate Library

◉ DID YA KNOW?

CAMPUS URBAN LEGENDS

The **Eternal Flame**, which is actually a light on the Quad, supposedly seals the fate of romantic couples on campus. Even if a "lover's kiss will bring eternal bliss" isn't true, many do choose to kiss here in hopes of prolonging their love.

The **Undergrad Library** was allegedly built underground because the Morrow Plots needed unimpeded sunlight. There are more aesthetic reasons for the UGL's subsurface location, but this is what is most often circulated.

Rats and mice are rumored to inhabit the basement of **Lincoln Hall**. Although the historic landmark is in dire need of repair, most of these tales are fabricated. After all, the only people who venture down there are a few TAs and maintenance workers.

◉ TOP 12 UNIVERSITY WEB ADDRESSES

Home Page with Most Pertinent Information: www.uiuc.edu

Registration and Records: https://apps.uillinois.edu/selfservice

Express E-mail Application: https://login.express.cites.uiuc.edu

Campus Map: www.uiuc.edu/ricker/CampusMap

Gen Ed Requirements: http://courses.uiuc.edu/cis/gened/urbana/2007/Fall

Registered Student Organizations:
www.union.uiuc.edu/involvement/rso/Default.aspx

General Events Calendar:
http://webtools.uiuc.edu/calendar/Calendar?calId=7

Phonebook Gateway: http://webtools.uiuc.edu/ows/PH

Library: www.library.uiuc.edu

Course Information: http://courses.uiuc.edu/cis/index.html

The Daily Illini Campus Newspaper: www.dailyillini.com

UIUC Compass Homework Site:
https://icprodportal01.cites.uiuc.edu/login.html

BLAH, BLAH

● RANDOM FACTS

— In addition to serving as the football team's home field, Memorial Stadium hosted the first Farm Aid concert (1985) and the Chicago Bears (2002) when Soldier Field was undergoing renovations.

— One of the most wired campuses in the world, UIUC has produced the founders of AMD, Netscape, Oracle, PayPal, Siebel Systems and YouTube.

— The world's first Web browser, Mosaic, was developed by the university's National Center for Supercomputing Applications (NCSA) in the early 1990s.

— The world's fastest supercomputer, "Blue Waters," which will cost $208 million, is being produced at the university and should go online in 2011. It will be capable of 1,000-trillion operations per second.

— Former physics professor John Bardeen is the only person to date to have won two Nobel Prizes for Physics. Bardeen won in 1956 for his work on the transistor and again in 1972 for his superconductivity theory.

— The Assembly Hall is one of the largest edge-supported structures in the world at around 400 feet wide.

— Pulitzer Prize–winning film critic and Urbana native Roger Ebert is an alumnus of the university. So is Playboy founder Hugh Hefner. Both worked for the school's independent student newspaper, The *Daily Illini*.

NUMBERS TO HAVE ON SPEED DIAL

C-U MTD: **(217) 384-8188**

SafeRides: **(217) 333-3184**

Campus information: **(217) 333-INFO**

WANT TO CHECK OUT WHAT OTHER CGUIDES ARE AVAILABLE?

Visit our website at
www.cguides.net

FIND OUT THE LATEST WHERE-TO-GO AND WHAT-TO-KNOW
INFORMATION FOR THE UNIVERSITY OF ILLINOIS
http://uiuc.cguides.net

RANK THE BEST PIZZA

POST A CAMPUS EVENT

LOOK FOR COUPONS AND DEALS

CHECK OUT WHAT'S HAPPENING

AND SO MUCH MORE!